OGILVIE'S ACT OF COWARDICE

Recent Titles by Philip McCutchan from Severn House

The James Ogilvie Series

THE FIRST COMMAND
SOLDIER OF THE QUEEN
CAPTAIN AT ARMS
HONOUR AND EMPIRE
OGILVIE AT WAR
OGILVIE UNDER FIRE
OGILVIE'S ROYAL COMMAND
OGILVIE AND THE MULLAH
OGILVIE AND THE TRAITOR
OGILVIE'S ACT OF COWARDICE

OGILVIE'S
ACT OF COWARDICE

Philip McCutchan

severn
House

This title first published in Great Britain 2002 by
SEVERN HOUSE PUBLISHERS LTD of
9–15 High Street, Sutton, Surrey SM1 1DF.
Originally published 1978 as *Charge of Cowardice*
under the pseudonym *Duncan MacNeil.*
This title first published in the USA 2002 by
SEVERN HOUSE PUBLISHERS INC of
595 Madison Avenue, New York, N.Y. 10022.

British Library Cataloguing in Publication Data

McCutchan, Philip, 1920-
    Ogilvie's act of cowardice. - (A James Ogilvie novel)
    1.   Great Britain. Army - History - 19th century - Fiction
    2.   Ogilvie, James (Fictitious character) - Fiction
    3.   India - History - 19th century - Fiction
    4.   Historical fiction
    I.   Title
    823.9'14 [F]

    ISBN 0-7278-5826-2

Printed and bound in Great Britain by
MPG Books Ltd., Bodmin, Cornwall.

One

EARLY JANUARY ON the North-West Frontier of India: a blood-red sun hung hugely through the afternoon haze, beginning to sink below the stark Afghan hills beyond the Khyber. A cold wind swept the parade-ground of the Royal Strathspey's cantonment, blowing out the Union Flag from its staff like a White Ensign blown from a battleship's main peak in a Channel gale; a snow-chilled wind that blew below the kilts of a defaulters' squad doubling with rifles held aloft to the raucous shouts of a drill-sergeant who was doubling himself to keep out the cold.

The shouted orders, the slam-slam-slam of heavy ammunition-boots, filled the barrack square and penetrated to the warm comfort of the Officers' Mess ante-room where James Ogilvie sat on the leather-seated fender warming his backside against the fire's red glow. At one end of the ante-room, beneath a large portrait of Her Majesty the Queen in lace cap and bun and haughty expression, sat Captain Black in animated conversation, over tea and wafer-thin bread-and-butter, with Major Lord Brora, second-in-command of the battalion, but recently appointed in the room of John Hay, deceased: killed, to be precise, in action and with honour. Ogilvie's expression, as he looked towards the Adjutant and the second-in-command, was sardonic: a Pathan bullet, fired from a long-barrelled *jezail*, had ended John Hay's life some three months earlier when the Major had ridden with the battalion into a Waziri ambush; Andrew Black had shown sorrow and concern, to be sure, but afterwards there had been a new springiness in his step, a lightening of his scowling moodiness. Naturally,

5

the whole battalion knew why; and there had been much festering, much muttering in the barrack-rooms as the acting 2 i/c had strutted the cantonment after the body of a popular if unspectacular Major had been consigned to the hard winter earth of Peshawar. As the pipes and drums had played the companies back from the military cemetery to cantonments, Black had ridden his horse alongside the Colonel and the look on his saturnine face had said clearly he expected his two captain's stars to be replaced at any moment by a major's crown. He was, after all, the senior captain in the battalion; his expectancy was natural enough. But it was not to be fulfilled. For two full days after the news had come through Andrew Black drowned his sorrows in whisky, managing only by the grace of God to appear sober in the Colonel's view: Major Lord Brora, commanding the regimental depot in far-off Invermore in the Monadliath Mountains, was under orders to join the battalion as second-in-command...

Ogilvie watched the animated conversation, the raising of the tea-cups to heavily moustached lips. Lord Brora was not unlike the Adjutant in appearance — tall, thin, black moustache, swarthy complexion. There the likeness ended: Brora was a Scots aristocrat, a laird, as was the Colonel, with a long tradition of army service behind him, while Black, English on his mother's side, came from trade — moneyed trade. Black was a wealthy man. As to the rest of it, time would tell. Brora had the reputation of being a hard man and a disciplinarian, and it was known that he had asked for a posting to the foreign-service battalion in the expectation of seeing action against the Pathan hordes. The apparent friendship was surprising: Ogilvie, perhaps uncharitably but with long knowledge of Andrew Black, put it down to arse-creeping on Black's part. The chances were that Brora had seen through it already: the new Major had a cold eye and a clear head.

Ogilvie left the fender and the ante-room, taking up his Sam Browne belt and glengarry from the hook outside in the corridor. Bound for the company office where the uncongeniality of paper-work awaited him, he crossed the square and returned the salute of the drill-sergeant and the eyes-right of the doubling unfortunates with their aching arms. Outside the office block he encountered the Regimental Sergeant-Major, who delivered a quivering salute accompanied by a stamp of boots as he halted.

"Good afternoon, Mr Cunningham."

"Captain Ogilvie, sir." The warrant officer's voice was muted well below its normal level. "There are rumours, sir. Maybe you'll have heard?"

Ogilvie smiled. "I haven't, I'm sorry to say. What rumours?"

"Movement orders, sir."

"For home, Sar'nt-Major?"

"Not for home, sir. For the south, sir. To Southern Command at Ootacamund, on temporary attachment.'

"Pure bush telegraph, Sar'nt-Major," Ogilvie said with a touch of impatience.

"Maybe so, sir. Time will tell." Cunningham gave a cough. "There's another matter, Captain Ogilvie, and this is no rumour: I've just visited the detention cells at Brigade, sir. The man Sudak Khan—he's sick. It's a matter for the Colonel, of course, but—"

"For the Colonel?" Ogilvie raised his eyebrows. "Sudak Khan's outside the Colonel's jurisdiction now. He's been passed to Brigade, hasn't he?"

Cunningham's voice became more formal. "With respect, Captain Ogilvie, he has not, other than in a physical sense. As one of our attached *syces,* sir, he remains a regimental commitment until sentence is executed. It will be for Surgeon Major Corton to attend, sir."

"If you say so, Sar'nt-Major. You'll inform the Colonel, then?"

"I will, sir, through Captain Black." Cunningham gave another swinging salute and stamped his feet in a left turn before marching away smartly, head high, chest out, pace-stick rigid beneath an immaculate arm. Ogilvie carried

7

on into the company office and started on the inevitable paper-work demanded of a company commander however good his clerk. He worked with only half his mind on the job in hand: rumour was merely rumour but was so often proved true, and Southern Command would make a change, a new part of India to be enjoyed, new scenery, new people to meet. Ogilvie thought also about death and the changes it brought: John Hay's loss, and the murder that had led to Sudak Khan's trial by Court Martial and the subsequent sentence of death. Some weeks earlier Sudak Khan, one of a number of *syces* on permanent secondment from an Indian cavalry regiment for the grooming of the battalion's horses, had killed a fellow *syce* by the exercise of *thuggee* after a dispute about a woman . . . and now was sick. Ogilvie gave a sigh; it would be more merciful to let the fellow die now than merely to preserve him for the firing squad or the hangman.

*   *   *

Next morning there was more unwelcome news, though its advent blew no ill wind towards Captain Black. Major Lord Brora sent runners to all the battalion's officers, plus the RSM, requesting their immediate attendance in the ante-room.

"I have grievous news, gentlemen," he said in a loud voice when the assembly was complete. "The Colonel met with an accident late last night, whilst riding back from Division at Nowshera. A fall from his horse—concussion, and a broken leg. He was found and taken back to the base hospital at Nowshera. He will be some weeks on the sick list." Lord Brora pulled back his shoulders, his hands behind his back, and stiffened his massive height—he was all of six foot three, which seemed to loft his granite jaw to almost flagpole level. "I am ordered by our Divisional Commander to assume the temporary command of the battalion. I am to remain in my rank of major, but in all respects I am your

8

Colonel and this you shall remember. Also temporarily, Captain Black will act as my second-in-command. Understood, Captain Black?" His eagle eye, seeking Black's face, stared down the heavy nose as he held his head arrogantly back.

"Yes, indeed, Colonel," Black said.

"You also will remain in your present rank." Black inclined his head obediently and offered no comment. "Captain Ogilvie, you will act as Adjutant in addition to your duties as B Company Commander."

"Yes, Major."

"Colonel."

"I'm sorry— Colonel."

Lord Brora lit a cigar and blew a cloud of smoke. "You may be assured, gentlemen, that I am fully aware of the reputation of this battalion under Lord Dornoch— a reputation of the finest, the very finest. Nevertheless, even the very finest can be improved upon." A hint of belligerence had crept into the new Colonel's tone, some quality almost of threat. "I am Lord Brora. Never in my life have I accepted less than the best. I intend to bring the battalion to the highest peak of efficiency, such that we shall stand out as the finest jewel in Her Imperial Majesty's military crown— no less! Captain Black?"

"Colonel?"

"You will permit, and Captain Ogilvie will permit, no slackness anywhere. You have been an action battalion ever since you first came to India, and this fact I honour. You are foremost in battle, but those who are foremost in battle are not always foremost in cantonments or on parade. Until events send us into action again, we shall become foremost in cantonments. Mr Cunningham?"

Cunningham got to his feet, back like a ramrod. "Sir!"

"You are the Regimental Sergeant-Major, the backbone of discipline. There will be no slackness in dress, in the giving of marks of respect, in the men's bearing upon parade, in personal cleanliness, in the barrack-rooms, when walking-out of cantonments. Et cetera. Do you understand me, Sar'nt-Major?"

"I do, sir. But with respect, sir, if I may—"

"Do you presume to answer me back, Sar'nt-Major?" Lord Brora's voice had grown louder. "Is this what you mean to do?"

"By no means, sir!"

"I'm dashed glad to hear it. I'm relieved! You may sit down, Sar'nt-Major."

Cunningham sat down rapidly, his face a picture. Ogilvie could almost feel his thoughts: never in all his service had he been accused, even by way of innuendo, of permitting slackness! Sweat could be seen running down Cunningham's face and into the collar of his khaki tunic. Meanwhile Lord Brora was continuing. "Captain Black, Captain Ogilvie, you shall go into conference with me immediately, and we shall set about our plans for improvements. Later, I shall have a personal word with the NCOs, the drill-sergeants in particular." He waved his cigar. "Thank you, gentlemen. The rest of you may carry on and I shall not expect to see any of you taking your ease here in the ante-room until luncheon. Sar'nt-Major, you'll remain. Oh, and you, Dr Corton, if you please. The matter of the sick *syce* in custody."

Surgeon Major Corton, sitting with legs crossed, nodded.

Brora glared. "Stand, if you please, when being addressed on duty. I am your Colonel, am I not?"

Corton's face reddened, but he got to his feet. "My apologies, Colonel," he said stiffly.

"Thank you, I accept your apology, Dr Corton." Brora pulled at his moustache. "I shall repeat myself: the *syce,* Sudak Khan under sentence of death. I understand he's sick. Your report, if you please."

Corton said, and Ogilvie sensed his relief in being able to say it, "I visited the man last evening, on getting word from Captain Black. He's sick all right, Colonel. Malnutrition . . . he refuses to eat."

"Why?"

10

Corton shrugged. "I think he sees little point, and prefers, since he is to die, to die in his own way."

"Tiresome."

"I beg your pardon, Colonel?"

"I said tiresome, Doctor. These natives are a dashed nuisance. Make him eat."

"Colonel, I—"

"An order, Doctor. The man's to eat. The food's to be forced down—or up! I understand there are methods of forcible feeding via the use of the enema tube. You shall employ it if necessary."

"Colonel—"

"That will be all, thank you." Pointedly Lord Brora turned aside, tweaking at one end of his heavy moustache, his eyes icy blue. Breathing hard, Surgeon Major Corton went out of the ante-room in the wake of the company officers. Brora, in a harsh voice, began laying down his plans; what followed was not so much a conference as a taking down of dictation. It was all done in quick time, but the audience left with their orders firmly rammed into their heads. At the door Black was recalled: Ogilvie noted the obsequious look in his face as he turned to go back. The new second-in-command, so fortuituously granted his dearest wish, was going to prove most sedulous to his Colonel's whims.

*   *   *

"A word, Captain Ogilvie, sir, if I may."

The encounter, not a chance one, was outside the door of the company office. Smiling, Ogilvie said, "Of course. And I think I know what about—right, Bosom?"

The use of his regimental nickname seemed to put Cunningham at his ease. "I've a strong wish to blow off steam, Captain Ogilvie, that's what!"

"Natural! We're old campaigners, Bosom. But shout softly!"

There was a happier look in Cunningham's eye, almost a

11

twinkle. "What's His Lordship at, sir, may I ask? There's none as smart as us, and he must know it!"

"It's the new broom, Sar'nt-Major, nothing more than that. Given time, the bristles will soften. And remember this: up to a point, he's right. We've seen a lot of action, and in the field considerations of dress and so on go by the board—"

"Aye, sir, and rightly too."

"But not in cantonments. And we've never been barrack-stanchions, I know that. One of the things the army's taught me is that the fighting units never have so much spit-and-polish about them as the ones that serve their time in cantonments— at least, not until they've settled down to barrack routine again. Am I not right?"

"Not entirely, sir. Not in our case."

"Spoken like an RSM," Ogilvie said with a smile. "There's been no reflection on you, Sar'nt-Major, that hasn't shone off the rest of us too. Take it in your stride, that's my advice— and slay it with the sharp end of your pace-stick!"

Cunningham nodded, saluted and turned about looking a shade less feather-ruffled. But as he marched away the swirl of the tartan around his knees seemed to suggest that a good use for the kilt might well be to smother Lord Brora, and the slam, bang of his boots on the parade-ground sounded to Ogilvie as if righteous indignation were treading down the earth on Lord Brora's grave. And that night in the Mess, after a gruelling day's drill and inspections, the soft lamplight, falling upon the regimental silver and the scarlet jackets and the white cotton gloves of the waiters, fell also upon moody officers, largely silent as they brooded upon the change of command and hoped, inwardly, that it would prove very temporary indeed. Though by custom shop was not spoken in the Mess, the ante-room after dinner held many small groups of disconsolate gossipers with only Andrew Black, making free with the whisky in his hour of glory as in his previous hour of gloom, looking happy and almost jovial.

Next morning came further change: Cunningham and his bush telegraph had been proved right; the battalion received orders from Division to move south.

Two

IT WAS VERY much as predicted by the Regimental Sergeant-Major: the 114th Highlanders, The Queen's Own Royal Strathspeys, were to leave for Coimbatore, below Ootacamund in the Nilgiri Hills, entraining in seven days' time. Lord Brora, after passing the movement order to his officers, ordered the battalion to be paraded so that he could address all ranks. As the companies began to assemble, four privates under a lance-corporal staggered to the centre of the parade-ground bearing the brass-railed dais that was normally brought out only for an inspecting general officer to take the salute at a march past. Lord Brora's own physical height was of itself adequate enough; the dais merely gilded the lily. The acting Colonel made a superbly impressive figure as he climbed the steps, his kilt blowing around his knees, and stood with his hands clasped behind his back and head held high, staring down at the assembled battalion. When the reports were all made, Lord Brora, returning Black's punctilious salute, said, "Thank you, Captain Black. Stand the parade at ease."

Black turned upon his heel, smartly, and roared out the order. Turning again, he faced the acting Colonel and stood himself at ease with a crash of his left foot.

"You men," Lord Brora said. He had no appearance of shouting, but his voice reached every far corner of the barrack square, like low thunder. He paused. "Captain Ogilvie?"

Ogilvie came to attention and saluted. "Colonel?"

"I gave the order, stand at ease. Not easy. You have a man lolling about like a drunk at a wedding."

"I'll have his name taken, Colonel—"

"Not necessary. I have eyes, Captain Ogilvie. The man is Private MacGarry. He is to be paraded at next Defaulters. Now we shall waste no more time." Lord Brora proceeded with his exposition of the movement order, leaving Ogilvie to marvel that any officer should, after so short a time with the battalion, be able to name an individual on parade. "I am ordered to join Her Majesty's Fourth Division under Major-General Sir Clarence Farrar-Drumm. The battalion will form part of a brigade to be temporarily exchanged with a brigade from Southern Command who will do Frontier duty in our stead. The battalion will be brigaded with the 2nd battalion the Border Regiment from Waziristan and a native battalion of the Indian Army—the 43rd Madras Light Infantry at present serving in Nowshera." Lord Brora rose and fell upon his heels for a space, staring down at the battalion. "A word about Sir Clarence Farrar-Drumm. He is a disciplinarian as I am myself. He is a man of much experience of command whose regimental days were spent with the Fourth Dragoon Guards. He has a passion for smartness, for efficiency, for dedication to duty. Now, you men will not want to let Lord Dornoch down in his absence—I know that. As for me, I am Lord Brora." The head went back even farther. "I shall ensure that you do not let *anyone* down. The slightest slackness will bring immediate retribution." He paused once again. "I understand that the action experience of our newly-formed brigade may quite speedily be put to the test, since Southern Command is facing disturbances originating in the district of Rangapore, whose damn Rajah is said to be growing weary of subjection to the princely state of Hyderabad. You may ask why we are replacing troops already there, rather than adding to them. I answer that it is not desired by the Civilians to exacerbate possible revolt along the border of the Madras Presidency, to add fuel to the flames that are blowing from Rangapore by being seen to strengthen the total force. Therefore a brigade—a *soft* brigade—is being detached and sent up

15

here, and while here will be hardened into soldiers. We are hard already, and that in itself is a reinforcement. That is all I have to say. Captain Black?"

"Colonel?"

"Carry on, if you please."

Black saluted and turned about to bring the parade to attention. In the silence left by the crash of boots and rattle of rifles being snapped back to the order position, Lord Brora stalked off parade towards his quarters, left hand resting on the hilt of his Highland broadsword. When he had gone more orders were passed and to the shouts of the NCOs the men were marched away by companies. Ogilvie was overtaken by the RSM and addressed in his acting rôle of Adjutant.

"Orders, Captain Ogilvie, sir?"

"General preparation, if you please, Mr Cunningham. Quartermasters to muster and check all stores, colour-sar'nts to check rifles and equipment. Company officers to see to kit inspections and all deficiencies made good before we entrain. Additional orders to follow when I've talked to the Colonel and Captain Black." He smiled. "Damn it, you know the drill better than I do!"

Cunningham didn't comment on that. He appeared to change the subject. He said, "The Colonel, sir, indicated that General Farrar-Drumm was an officer of much command experience, did he not?"

"He did."

"There was something he did not say, sir."

Ogilvie stared. "Well, go on, Sar'nt-Major."

"Very good, sir." There was a curious gleam in Cunningham's eye. "When I joined the regiment, sir, which was back in '67 . . . General Farrar-Drumm was a Brigadier-General."

"Good God!" Ogilvie said involuntarily. "Are you sure?"

Cunningham nodded. "Aye, sir, I'm sure. The regiment was in garrison with his cavalry brigade, at Aldershot." He paused, took a deep breath and blew it out again. "He's a very old gentleman, sir. Mind, he was young for his rank then, but . . ."

"But not now?"

"Not now, sir."

*　　　*　　　*

Old generals were not *ipso facto* bad generals, but there did tend to be a certain rigidity of mind as the arteries hardened; and the prospect of action under the aegis of a Divisional Commander even older than Bloody Francis Fettleworth was not a happy one. However, there was little time for contemplation of generals; the bustle and activity involved in the movement, the long journey by train into the Madras Presidency, were considerable. Along with its horses, mules and camels the regiment was taking, inevitably, its camp followers, the motley crowd of natives who dealt with the commissariat and the general housework of a march, and marching there would certainly be at some stage of their service with Southern Command. Since their posting was to be temporary, however, the wives and women "on the strength" were being left behind in their quarters; the Royal Strathspey's cantonment would be occupied by one of the regiments from Ootacamund who would also be leaving their women behind. If the married officers should wish to take their ladies, no official objection would be raised but the officers concerned would have to meet the expenses themselves. On this, however, Lord Brora had other views, personal ones that over-rode the official pronouncement. He proclaimed them in the ante-room a couple of days before departure.

"The ladies," he said, lighting a cigar and taking a glass of whisky from the Mess waiter. "Few of us are married, I know." He blew smoke, following the trail with his eye. "Dr Corton and Mr MacCrum, I think you in fact are the only married ones among us?"

"Correct, Colonel." Surgeon Major Corton folded his

17

copy of the *Times of India*. "My wife stays here—moving about is expensive."

"Yes, indeed." Lord Brora's hard stare rested upon the short, stout body of Lieutenant and Quartermaster MacCrum. "Mr MacCrum?"

"Mrs MacCrum wishes to accompany me, Colonel."

"Indeed?"

MacCrum said defensively, "The orders leave us the option, Colonel."

"Indeed," Brora said again, and sniffed.

"And she's not been well, Colonel."

"I see. Sickness is a fact of service, Mr MacCrum. So is absence, and it's to be but temporary. Mrs MacCrum remains in cantonments."

"But Colonel, the orders say—"

"The orders say, the orders say! In point of fact, Mr MacCrum, the orders *say* nothing at all, since they are written and are therefore inarticulate. I give not a fig for the orders on this occasion, and I think you will find, should you quote the orders at me again, that no order ever given will support disobedience to your Colonel, Mr MacCrum. Captain Black?"

"Colonel?"

Lord Brora took the rest of his *chota-peg* in a single gulp and set his empty glass down hard. "I find surly persons a bore, and most offensive. We are here to fight, not to fornicate. I shall go to my quarters, Captain Black."

"Yes, Colonel."

Brora strode towards the door, preceded by Black. At the door he turned, stared at the officers, and said, *"Bachelors* make the best officers. They have nothing to lose but their lives." He turned away. Black gave a kind of bow, reached past the tall figure of the acting Colonel, and held the door open politely. Turning back towards the others, he met cold looks and raised eyebrows at his unnecessary obsequiousness. Flushing darkly, he snapped his fingers at the waiter, demanding whisky.

18

The Surgeon Major caught MacCrum's eye and winked. "Never mind, Charlie. We all suffer in our different ways. I was given precise orders this morning: no man's to go on the sick list before we entrain."

"You'll not obey that, Doctor?"

Corton laughed. "Of course not!"

"But I've no option," Macrum said bitterly. "I'm no' a professional man, and I need my army pay." He mimicked the Colonel's voice: *"I am Lord Brora!* By Christ, if yon birkie's a colonel, then so's my arse."

*   *   *

By the time the farewell parade was fallen in, there was hardly an officer—apart, it seemed, from Black—or an NCO who had not suffered from Lord Brora's tongue and actions. Private MacGarry of the rank and file, found guilty at the Colonel's defaulters' table of slackness on parade, of being that terrible object an idle soldier, had been confined to barracks until departure and had spent many heavy hours doubling the square with his rifle and a full marching pack. Like MacCrum, RSM Cunningham, who was entitled to officers' privileges, had been forbidden to take his wife south. In regard to the women, the chattels of the married Other Ranks, everyone except Lord Brora realised a blunder had been made in so far as they were being left in cantonments earmarked for the occupation of another regiment: soldiers on long Indian service were never saints, and wives could stray when their menfolk were absent. Such an unimaginative move by the high command was going to be bad for morale. The barrack-rooms had seethed for days past; every man wished he were still under the command of Lord Dornoch, every man prayed for Dornoch's swift return to duty. The Colonel—as they all still thought of Dornoch and never mind Lord Brora—had been visited by all the officers and by the Regimental Sergeant-Major; he was still a sick man from the concussion and some other injury to the head, and his leg was heavy with plaster. He had wished them well, but obviously his heart was heavy at being left behind. From the visitors Lord Brora came in for scant mention; he was acting Colonel and officers were never disloyal. But many of those officers realised that Dornoch had read between the lines of silence, and was anxious about his regiment.

During the afternoon before departure from cantonments Brora had sent for the Surgeon Major, who found the Colonel in his quarters, standing with cigar and whisky before a long wall mirror, studying himself and thrusting out his jaw. Brora seemed not in the least abashed to be thus caught when his corporal of servants announced the doctor.

He swung round. "Ah yes, Dr Corton." He waited until the corporal had withdrawn. "That *syce,* what's his name—"

"Sudak Khan."

"Yes. How's he making out?"

Corton shrugged. "There's been a little improvement, Colonel."

"The forcible feeding?"

"Yes."

"I see. He's to come with us."

"*What?*"

"I think you heard me, Doctor. The order's already been given. I've sent for you to tell you to make your arrangements, not to argue with me." Brora waved his cigar in the doctor's face. "An example, a very visible example to the men, also to the damn camp followers. Someone who's going to die for actions against the Raj and the regiment."

Corton snapped, "I find that quite scandalous, Colonel!"

"Indeed?" Brora raised his eyebrows. "You shall obey my orders nevertheless, at peril of your appointment."

"I do not believe Brigade will hand the man over to you, Colonel."

"Then you will be surprised, Doctor. I am Lord Brora. And I do not like damn natives. You will bring the enema tube."

                              *   *   *

The salute was taken by Brigadier-General Lakenham, Fettleworth's Chief-of-Staff who had come from Nowshera to wish the regiment God-speed. With him on the dais was Lord Brora, eyes flashing fire as the companies marched past in column of route behind the pipes and drums. The drums beat out in time to "A Hundred Pipers", savage, exultant, boastful; Brora's hand beat out as well, thumping the brass rail of the dais. Ogilvie, giving an eyes-left as his company marched past, noticed the Colonel's facial emotion, saw his lips moving.

> Oh, wha' is foremost o' a', o' a'?
> Oh, wha' does follow the blaw, the blaw?
> Bonnie Charlie, the king o' us a', hurrah!
> Wi' his hundred pipers an' a', an' a'!
> His bonnet an' feathers he's waving high,
> His prancing steed maist seems to fly!
> The nor' wind plays wi' his curly hair
> While the pipes blaw in an unco' flare!

All that was missing, since Brora would be prancing, steed-mounted within the next few minutes, was the curly hair . . . They marched away from cantonments to the continuing pipes and drums and the hoofbeats of the field officers' horses and the rumble of the transport and ammunition column and the sounds from the marching feet, waved away by the ladies and wives and women and by the men of the regiments from the other cantonments, cheering crowds that lined the long route in to the railway station where the regiment was met by the Border Regiment and the 43rd Madras Light Infantry, the latter going back to their home ground with their turbans and pantaloons, their puttees and bullet-filled bandoliers. It was a splendidly colourful scene, a military spectacle of khaki and red and blue, of green and white and gold, of decorations, medal

21

ribbons and orders. The departure for home or for service elsewhere in the great sub-continent of one of the family of British regiments was always an occasion, especially in the dull and largely bungalow-bound lives of the mem-sahibs. At last, to a forest of waving arms and a crescendo of cheering that almost overwhelmed the brass band on the platform, the three heavily-laden troop-trains pulled out and away from Peshawar. The journey south would be a long and slow one; the railway led through Rawalpindi and Amritsar, to Bhatinda, Bikaner, Bhilwara . . . down to Nander and Secunderabad, right on through the Madras Presidency, down to Bangalore, on across the Eastern Ghats for Salem and Coimbatore—a total distance as the crow flies of some sixteen hundred miles, but very much farther by the railway, and with many, many changes en route.

*   *   *

It was official winter, but it was hot as they dropped south to the level of Bombay and below: the shade temperature climbed to ninety in the open air, the crowded troop-trains grew correspondingly hotter and more stifling, filled with the smells of sweating bodies, basically unwashed as the long days went by, and of cooking food, and of tobacco. Men talked and quarrelled, slept, relieved themselves out of the windows, swatted at crawling flies and insects. At the junctions, some of them reached in the middle of the night, legs were stretched for a while as the trains were shunted this way and that. At these halts Ogilvie made a point of observing Sudak Khan, murderer: the native had been secured in a kind of cage constructed of bamboo, in which he lay sad-eyed on a heap of rags in a guard's van under the rifles and bayonets of a corporal and four privates—Lord Brora, having been granted his hand-over, was taking no chances of escape. The indignity of forcible feeding per rectum had continued, for Sudak Khan still refused to eat. The word of his presence, well enough known to the Scots,

22

had quickly spread to the remainder of the brigade in the other trains; and the men were mostly indifferent. The black bugger had killed and had himself to die; but many saw his presence as ghoulish and unnecessary, and Ogilvie, with Dr Corton, was one of these. The long days and nights dragged on; in the officers' coach conditions were more or less bearable, with *punkahs* stirring the air, and softly-cushioned seats, and food reasonably well served by the Mess waiters. In the compartment reserved for the battalion commanders there was even a degree of luxury: Lord Brora, with Colonel Hinde of the Border Regiment, the 34th and 55th Foot, and Colonel Wilkinson of the Madras Light Infantry, reclined in a splendour not far removed from that of the drawing-room coach used by Her Majesty when travelling by the royal train to Balmoral or upon visits of inspection to her army depots and naval dockyards. There were antimacassars adorning the chair-backs, and the chairs themselves were mounted on swivels for the convenience of their occupants when they wished to use the small tables for their drinks and meals and the paper-work brought by their attentive adjutants; or when they wished to sit and gaze through the ample windows at the unfolding wonders, wonders new to all the personnel except the men from Madras, of the southern half of the sub-continent: the trains carried them over tumultuous rivers of dirty brown water dotted with carcases human and animal, through enfolding green forests, across mighty open plains and through gentle slopes extending to high ranges of hills. Along the track from time to time natives watched, men and women halting in their labours to see the splendid British Raj pass by behind the heaving, steamy engines. Mostly the ragged peasants salaamed to the colourful enlargements of the regimental badges displayed on the engine fronts, to the brigade insignia, to the visible embodiment of the power and authority of the Queen-Empress stretching across the oceans from far-off Windsor Castle in the land of the White Gods; but some shook fists, or turned their backs. One of these Lord Brora saw, and gave acid tongue.

23

"Hinde, Wilkinson! Did you see that?"

"The fist in our faces?" It was the Madras Light Infantry-man who answered, smiling slightly but looking saddened. "I did. Love for us is not universal, my dear chap."

"Feller ought to be shot."

"And probably will be," Wilkinson said sombrely, "when the trouble breaks. We're into Hyderabad now, and well south. You know our likely orders, Brora."

"I shall enjoy carrying them out." Brora stared from the window, his blue eyes like glaciers, his mouth hard. "Why can't the buggers be grateful to us, and knuckle down like their fathers did?"

Wilkinson gave a dry chuckle. "As in the Mutiny?" he asked sardonically. "It's always been simmering. You wouldn't like Scotland to be occupied, Brora."

"A totally different thing!" Brora snapped. "We in Scotland are not black natives, incapable of managing our own affairs without assistance." He glared: his eagle eye had caught a look passing between Hinde and Wilkinson, had caught the gleam of honour that said so clearly that in fact Scotland was governed from Whitehall. Brora's face suffused; he said in a throaty voice, "I demand an apology . . . for what you have not said, but would wish to— if you dared, gentlemen!"

It was Colonel Hinde, senior of the three battalion commanders, who answered. "You have it, Brora. You have it in full. It was just a little passing persiflage, no more than that, a reflection upon your somewhat forthright words. I honour the Scots and their soldiers— none more so." He paused, stroking his chin. "I imagine you've not served in India until now, Brora?"

"I have not. South Africa, Bermuda, Malta. Why d'you ask, sir?"

Hinde shrugged. "You'll find India's quite different. It's a land of princes, more powerful and far, far wealthier than the Queen. That's worth bearing in mind." Before Lord Brora could react, another officer had joined the group: Brigadier-

24

General Masefield, the Brigade Commander. Masefield wished them good morning and bade them remain seated. It was, he said, time to finalise the arrangements for de-training; on the morrow they would arrive at Coimbatore and a message received by the telegraph at one of the en route railway stations had indicated that Sir Clarence Farrar-Drumm was to do the Brigade the honour of coming down from Ootacamund to meet them in person. The three Adjutants and the Regimental Sergeant-Majors—the *Havildar*-Major in the case of the native unit—were sent for and under the co-ordination of the Brigadier-General the detailed orders were compiled for the operation of de-training and assembling the three battalions and their stores, baggage, animals, weapons and equipment, and for the march, after the welcoming ceremonial, from the railway station to their allotted cantonments in garrison. The arrival through the tree-clad Nilgiri Hills was made on schedule next day, the troop-trains hauling singly, slowly and creakily into the station at Coimbatore, the leading one halting in a cloud of steam before a most splendid display of military and civil dignity. A red carpet had been laid to take the feet of Brigadier-General Masefield and his colonels, and the door of his carriage was stopped with much precision—after some backing and filling—at the edge of this carpet. To the left of the Brigadier-General's disembarkation point was the depot brass of an Indian infantry regiment together with the drums and fifes of the 41st and 69th Foot—the Welch Regiment from home—and the trumpets of the Deccan Horse; at the end of the red carpet the welcoming committee was assembled: high-ranking officers and their somewhat gaunt ladies, the Major-General and his staff, some black-coated Civilians, a handful of native officials, with the station master, an Anglo-Indian, hovering obsequious attendance upon the newly-arrived brass from the north. Ogilvie, walking past the Commanding Officers' coach in his rôle of acting Adjutant of the Royal Strathspeys, saw Lord Brora's cold stare at the station master and his mutter about damn

25

chi-chis. He saw Brora's gaze sweep the platform, taking in the floral decorations obviously freshly placed in welcome by an attentive station staff, taking in the motley hordes of low-caste natives at either end of the platform and spilling out onto the railway track. Then the bands were playing and a stately personage bearing upon his shoulders the crossed sword and baton, with star above, of a Major-General, advanced two paces ahead of the assembled brass: Major-General Sir Clarence Farrar-Drumm was a striking figure, as tall as Lord Brora, with a big leathery face emerging from behind snow-white hair. Hair sprouted from nostrils and ears; hair hung in vast side-whiskers like young bushes, joining an immense walrus moustache yellowed with cigar smoke. Below this moustache the mouth itself could not be seen, but the chin was large and square and out-thrust, cleaving cleanly between the proliferation of the dangling side-whiskers. Sir Clarence, a man of many campaign medals and other decorations, advanced with the aid of a stick and the assiduous arm of an aide-de-camp. As Cunningham had said, a very old gentleman.

"Ah, Masefield."

The Brigadier-General saluted smartly. "Sir!"

"Delighted to see you, very."

"I'm delighted to join your command, sir. May I present Lieutenant-Colonel Hinde, Lieutenant-Colonel Wilkinson, Major Lord Brora."

Salutes were exchanged and hands were shaken: Farrar-Drumm's hand seemed arthritic, and he winced as Brora grasped it. "Do be careful," he said angrily. "I'm no longer a young man."

"I'm sorry, sir."

The Major-General peered closely. "You're Brora?"

"Yes, sir."

"Knew yer father. Scots Guards. Why didn't you join 'em?" A spasm seized Sir Clarence, a violent fit of coughing that ended, after an embarrassing interval, in a curse against damn bronchitis. "Wouldn't have you, I dare say. They didn't like yer father much, come to think of it." He turned again to the Brigadier-General. "You look hot and dusty. I suggest you come with me in my carriage . . ." His voice trailed away and a puzzled look entered his eyes.

The ADC came to his General's assistance. "You're mounted today, sir. *Riding,* sir."

"Ah—so I am, so I am, to be sure! When your horse is ready, Masefield, we'll ride to Brigade for a *chota-peg.* No doubt your battalion commanders can march their men into cantonments without your presence."

"Thank you, sir." Masefield saluted. His horse was brought speedily from the horse-truck, checked by the farrier-sergeant and the veterinary officer, and saddled up. Then the assembly moved out of the station to the concourse, where the Major-General's escort waited, his horse being held by a *syce.* A mounting-block was brought and with some difficulty Sir Clarence was guided into his saddle, where he sat coughing and panting, his leathery face temporarily scarlet. Then, as Masefield brought his own horse alongside and the mounted escort, found by a detachment of the Deccan Horse, formed up, there came a high scream from the station platform behind, followed by a low but rising murmur from the Untouchables crowding the track.

Three

I<small>T HAPPENED TO</small> be the 114th Highlanders who stood between the source of the trouble and the officers and ladies of the welcoming committee: Ogilvie reacted fast, calling out to the company commanders as Black stood looking irresolute. The Scots, under Ogilvie's orders, formed a solid barrier to hold back the native mob on the railway track. The natives hesitated, bunching as those behind pressed on and the leaders gazed into the rifle-mouths of the Royal Strathspeys. Then an outflanking movement began, the rearmost natives running round behind the stationary troop-train to come up at its end where the men of the Border Regiment had been disembarked from the waiting second train to hold the platform.

Lord Brora strode up to Ogilvie, moustache seeming to bristle. "You, there. You, sir! Captain Ogilvie, what the devil are you doing?"

"Holding off the mob, Colonel—"

"The devil you are. They're going round the other side!"

"Into the rifles of the Border Regiment, Colonel."

"Don't you damn well argue with me, Captain Ogilvie. Why the devil didn't you open fire, man?"

"And cause a massacre, Colonel?"

"On the contrary—prevent one. You'll open upon them at once, upon their front ranks, and see that they turn their backsides to you, d'you hear me?"

"Yes, Colonel." Ogilvie turned about, found the RSM at his side. "Over their heads, Sarn't-Major."

"Sir!" Cunningham saluted, turned on his heel, and roared

28

out the order. The Scots rifles opened in flame and a reek of gunsmoke; bullets sped over the native heads. The mob turned and ran, the leaders now following their rear ranks around the cover of the train. Stones and debris flew back over the coaches, hitting the British soldiers and Civilian officials, clattering on the platform. The yelling continued; back onto the platform came Sir Clarence Farrar-Drumm, riding his horse straight through the booking hall and out towards the mêlée, where he sat surveying the scene, his face like thunder. He saw something that caused him further fury: the native, Sudak Khan, who had been deposited earlier on the platform in his cage of stout bamboo.

"What's that, may I ask?" He pointed with his riding crop.

The Brigadier-General explained. "Permission to bring the man was asked by the Colonel of the 114th, sir, and given by Brigade in Peshawar."

"By you?"

"Not by me, sir. Before my brigade was formed."

"But you consented."

". . . d, sir, though I knew nothing of the cage."

"Then you should have!" Sir Clarence snapped. "It's a damn disgrace and it's obvious to me it's been the cause— or anyway the spark— that it's touched off this damn riot!" He swivelled dangerously in his saddle, turning this way and that. "Provost-Marshal! Where's my Provost-Marshal . . . oh, there you are, Coles."

"Sir!"

"Clear the platform— get the blasted women to hell out, *and* the Civilians— have the trains pulled away to deny those buggers their cover. Then disperse them with rifle fire. A few corpses and the rest'll run to save their own dirty hides."

"Very good, sir."

"Use your military police, Coles. I'm far from impressed with the line troops." As the Provost-Marshal saluted and went about his orders, Sir Clarence turned on the Brigadier-General. "Yes, far from impressed. You were sent here to stiffen Southern Command— first-class regiments straight from border action, I was told." He sniffed. "If you ask me, you were taken off your guard."

"No, sir." Masefield swept a hand around the platform as the primitive missiles continued coming over the train's roof. "Both ends are held, sir, and held well. There's not one native gained access to the platform."

The General glared. "I don't like argumentative officers, Masefield. When I state a fact, a fact it becomes, do you understand? You were taken off your guard. In due course I shall have a word with you and your battalion commanders."

A moment later the firing began: with the Scots deployed around one end and the Borderers at the other, the native regiment held the centre. As the trains chuffed out in their clouds of smoke and steam, the military police moved in with rifles, forming a firing-line at the platform's edge in advance of the infantrymen and then jumping down in pursuit of the mob as it turned and fled. Half a dozen bleeding corpses were left behind, together with a number of wounded natives who were arrested and dragged to their feet to be marched to the town jail. It was, Ogilvie thought, an unpleasant welcome to Coimbatore. Leaving the Provost-Marshal and his men to tidy up, the regiments were fallen in outside the station and marched away to cantonments behind the fifes and drums of the Borderers. Never mind the recent shooting: here, as in Peshawar, the roads were lined with cheering soldiers and their families, the latter waving Union Flags as the battle-experienced men from Northern Command and the Frontier marched into garrison.

*   *   *

The ante-room was comfortable, but it was not home: home was in the Peshawar cantonment. Enough of home had been brought to assuage nostalgia, however, and packing-cases littered the middle of the room as the Mess silver was brought from its wrappings of green baize together with some of the more transportable pictures donated by the

30

members of the Mess from time to time during their Indian service. Not all were of India: some were of Scotland; and, looking at these in new surroundings, Ogilvie was visited by a sudden yearning to see the mountains again, and the lochs, and the glens, and the wild roads winding through the heather that empurpled the Highlands. He thought of the stormy Forth and the trains making their way over the great bridge from Edinburgh as they hauled their passengers and freight through all weathers to Inverness and beyond; he thought of the wild wind blowing the waters of the Firth of Clyde into white horses, of a full gale screaming past the hills of Arran to blow spray over the lighthouse at Toward Point outside Rothesay Bay; and thought of the great castle of Corriecraig and the lands of his fathers. It was not possible to think of Ogilvie and Corriecraig as separate; and for a long time now the 114th Highlanders had also been a part, and an important part, of the pattern. His grandfather Sir Malcolm had commanded in his time; his father, Sir Iain, had commanded before his promotion to general's rank and was even now the Lieutenant-General Commanding, Northern Army, opposite number to Sir Clarence Farrar-Drumm and as different from that old gentleman as was chalk from cheese, though it had to be confessed that he had his share of any general officer's testiness and autocracy . . .

Ogilvie turned from the picture— it happened to be a print of the Tay rushing in tumult below General Wade's Bridge at Aberfeldy in Perthshire— that had projected his mind across the seas. He met the eye of Robin Stuart, commanding E Company, and grinned at him.

"There's a different feel, isn't there, Robin?"

Stuart nodded. "Yes. Funny . . . it's all basically the same."

"So's any garrison, but each has its differences— subtle, but noticeable. They have an easier life down here than on the Frontier— that's what you can feel, I think. It's in the atmosphere." Ogilvie wrinkled his nose. "A lack of immediacy, perhaps?"

"I think that's it. A lack of alarums and excursions—or a lack of the feeling they're likely." Stuart pulled out a pipe and a tobacco-pouch and dropped into an armchair, swinging a leg over one of the arms. "Brora—the Colonel I should say—spoke of incipient rebellion or some such, and I must say that was a pretty ugly scene at the railway station. We may be in for some fun." He paused, flame hovering over the filled bowl of his pipe. "I hear rumour that the Colonel's been carpeted."

"Oh?"

"Over the caging of that *syce.*" Stuart blew a cloud of smoke. "Farrar-Drumm almost had a fit. He sent for the Colonel to wait upon him at Brigade—where his tones were very loudly heard indeed and his sentiments duly passed on. Apparently our respected Colonel's being blamed for exacerbating native emotions. Corton was called in and condemned the whole damn shooting-match. Brora's not happy, I'm told."

"And the *syce?*"

Stuart shrugged. "Well, he has to be kept alive, Farrar-Drumm was in agreement on that point. You can't just let the condemned die—I suppose there's a certain logic—"

"Is there?"

Stuart lifted an eyebrow. "Yes, James. When a date's set for the convenience of all concerned, the guilty man is still, pro tem, a living entity. He has to play his part, what's more—"

"And not spoil the show?"

"Eh?"

"I think you heard," Ogilvie answered shortly. "I—" He broke off as footsteps beat loudly along the verandah. The ante-room door opened and Black strode in, heavy-faced, halting as he saw the seated officers.

"Captain Stuart, kindly stop lounging like an off-duty waiter. Captain Ogilvie, are you acting Adjutant, or are you not?"

32

"A rhetorical question, I take it," Ogilvie said calmly.

Black's face darkened and he slapped his cane against his trews. "Be about your business, Captain Ogilvie! You—"

"I have been about my business, Captain Black. The battalion is settled into cantonments and the details may quite safely be left now to the RSM and the RQMS."

"That may be so. You know very well the Colonel objects to company officers skrimshanking in the ante-room. You will go out and supervise—as a company commander, not as Adjutant." There was a smirk on Black's face now. "I have news for you, my dear Ogilvie. *I* am in fact to resume my proper function as Adjutant, in addition to my duties as second-in-command. The Colonel considers you need further company experience—he was far from satisfied with your conduct at the railway station this morning."

"In what way?"

Black swished his cane. "Slow reactions to a menacing situation, and a failure to fire into the mob when ordered. It was left to the General to give the order himself. And now here is another order."

"Well?"

"The *syce*, Sudak Khan. He is to be executed tomorrow, but it is not to be a regimental parade. The General has ordered him to be hanged in the civil jail at eleven a.m. Your company is to provide the escort, Captain Ogilvie." Black turned and stalked out of the ante-room. Ogilvie and Stuart exchanged glances; Stuart, shrugging, got to his feet, left the room and marched across the barrack square. Ogilvie made his way across behind him, heading for the armoury where he would find his colour-sergeant, MacTrease. His expression was bleak. Already there was a sour note in the move south. In the armoury he gave MacTrease the order for the next day's escort into the town and the civil jail.

"Full alertness, Colour MacTrease."

"Aye, sir. After this morning—that's what you're thinking, sir?"

Ogilvie nodded. "Yes. No chances."

"Would not a covered commissariat wagon be more prudent, sir?"

"We'll not question the orders, Colour MacTrease."

"Sir!" MacTrease stamped his boots in a quivering salute and Ogilvie left the armoury to take a look at his company's barrack-room. MacTrease, in fact, had been absolutely right; Ogilvie saw in the orders for an escort of company strength a sop to Lord Brora: ordered to execute his man speedily and in the privacy of the town jail rather than continue to hold him as an object lesson, he was not being deprived entirely of an ostentatious despatch. Sir Clarence was evidently a man of some tact, if possibly misplaced on this occasion.

That night in Mess and ante-room Ogilvie was pre-occupied: he had no liking for death marches, for the cruel ceremonial that took a condemned man to the gallows. On one previous occasion, in the Peshawar cantonment, he had witnessed a public hanging: a corporal of the regiment who had deliberately shot an officer. It had been impossible, afterwards, to eradicate the scene from his mind. The regiment drawn up in hollow square, the mournful wailing of the pipes, the beat of the crêpe-draped drums as the man had been marched by his escort around the parade so that every soldier could witness dishonour and the enduring of a man's last moments upon earth: a dreadful march that had ended in the murderer being halted by his ready coffin until the scaffold was ready for him. It had seemed like pure sadism, and it seemed so still. At least the next day's business would include no seeing of the hanging. As Ogilvie sipped an after-dinner brandy in the ante-room with Robin Stuart for company, Black approached.

"Ah, James." The use of the christian name indicated an intended friendliness on the part of Black, which was something. "A word, if I may . . . no, no, I'll not sit, thank you, I have matters to attend to. I wish just to tell you this: the Major-General would like you to call upon him— he was once well acquainted with your father, and has expressed an interest through the Colonel."

"Right, Andrew, I'll be delighted. When's it to be?"

"The sooner the better. I understand we shall not be long in cantonments—but no more of that for now. Not tomorrow. Sir Clarence leaves for Ootacamund during the time you'll be on escort duty. He suggests the next day . . . it's but fifty-odd miles, and there is a mountain railway to take you up into the Nilgiri Hills." Black paused. "The Colonel will be pleased to allow you forty-eight hours' leave of absence, James."

Ogilvie raised his eyebrows. "Will I need that long?"

"If your business with Sir Clarence takes less time, you are of course free to return earlier." Black turned and walked away, his dress kilt swinging around skinny knees. Ogilvie had fresh food for thought now: "business with Sir Clarence" seemed to indicate that his forthcoming visit to Southern Army headquarters might in fact involve more than a simple chat about his family.

*   *   *

From an early pre-breakfast hour the escorting company had drilled under the eye of Colour-Sergeant MacTrease, standing imminently critical as his drill-sergeant chased and harried the private soldiers about the barrack square. After the first fifteen minutes, MacTrease intervened, ordering a halt and a stand-at-ease as he marched forward with his pace-stick beneath his arm. From his room, Ogilvie heard the Colour-Sergeant's voice raised in loud complaint that ended thus:

"What's the bloody *matter* wi' you? You dinna ken so I'll tell you: too much bloody sitting aboot in the train, that's what! God give me strength to endure the bloody *sight* of you! Och, you're bone *idle*. You're no' soldiers, you're sacks o' horse manure. You'll smarten yourselves up, *if* you please! An' you'll remember this: you're no' just the escort for a condemned murderer and his death march,

35

you're seasoned troops from the North-West bloody Frontier and you're *Scots*. And you're going to impress bloody Coimbatore— *right?"*

No answer given, none expected: to have given an answer would have been to answer back. Simple obedience was all MacTrease wanted, and he got it. The marching was smarter, the backs straighter, the angle of the sloped rifles neared synchronised perfection. The Scots were going to put on a show for the benefit of such Southern Army troops as cared to learn a lesson.

And this they did.

At a few minutes past nine o'clock, after the Union Flag had been hoisted to the head of the flagstaff in the presence of the Colonel, the colour guard and a bugler, Ogilvie crossed the square to take command of the escort; his two subalterns were already marching up and down with drawn broadswords as the condemned *syce*, hands cuffed behind his back, was brought under armed personal escort from the cells and put into his place in the centre of B Company with two sections ahead of him and two more behind, with two pipers and two drummers in the lead. All reports made, Ogilvie was about to give the order to march when he was approached by a runner from the Colonel.

"Captain Ogilvie, sir— "

"What is it, Campbell?"

"The Colonel, sir. He'd like a word, sir."

"Very good." Ogilvie marched smartly across the square and halted in front of Lord Brora, who returned his salute with a somewhat belligerent air.

"Eyes skinned, Captain Ogilvie. The man's to be well guarded. You'll not hesitate— this time— to shoot."

"To shoot Sudak Khan, Colonel?"

The eyes glittered. "Kindly do not wilfully and insubordinately misunderstand, Captain Ogilvie. To use your rifles against any attempt to prevent the native's delivery at the jail."

"That is an order, Colonel?"

"Certainly it is an order. This is India, Captain Ogilvie. A word of caution, however: you are not to fail to distinguish between a deliberate attack upon the escort, and simple mob harassment. In other words, you will not open fire unless and until you are under attack. Clear?"

"As at the railway station yesterday, Colonel?"

Brora's face darkened. "I think, my dear sir, you are indulging in semasiology!"

"No, Colonel. With great respect, I ask for clarification of my orders. I submit that there was no actual ·attack at the railway station, so—"

"Stones and pieces of timber are missiles. The casting of missiles constitutes attack." Brora was furious; the fingers of his hands bunched, the knuckles stood out and he half lifted his cane as though about to strike. Then he controlled himself and said in a voice of ice, "You will not argue further. Go back to your company this instant."

Ogilvie saluted and turned about with a slam of boots and marched back towards the escort, angry himself. The Colonel's orders were still unclear: in Ogilvie's book, the casting of missiles picked from the streets, or from a railway track for that matter, constituted "simple mob harassment" and did not of itself call for retaliation by rifle fire: time enough for that when the mob moved in with obvious intent to kill—unless, of course, one wished to exacerbate a situation and provoke the attack so that the rifles could be used with justification! Lord Dornoch, Ogilvie knew well, would never countenance his regiment being used in such a manner. As he gave the order to quick march out of the cantonment, Ogilvie was well aware that he was about to tread a tightrope: word had already come through from the town's Provost-Marshal that the natives were gathering. He had in fact discussed before breakfast with Black the advisability of taking a less direct route to the jail, but Black had demurred strongly, talking much about the honour of the regiment and how it would appear to the Southern regiments and corps if a unit noted for its Frontier fighting

37

were, so soon in its posting, to be deflected by a native mob. "You'll have full backing from the regiments in garrison," Black had said. "The Provost-Marshal will be keeping the streets as clear as possible." But had added a warning concealed in a reasonable-seeming statement: "Naturally, it'll be up to you to make a last-minute decision in the light of what you find."

Black and Brora: two peas in a pod!

The pipes and drums played the prisoner and escort out through the barrack gate, where the Quarter-Guard and sentries saluted Ogilvie's passing. The tune, was *"Hey, Johnny Cope"*, a lively step, a disrespectful reference to the English general soundly defeated by Prince Charles Edward in the '45, to the extent that he had himself carried the news of his own defeat to Carlisle, having run so fast from action that he had outdistanced his own retreating troops after taking prudent precautions the night before, as a result of intelligence received of the Scottish strength. The words, pointed up now by the drums, beat into Ogilvie's mind:

> When Johnny Cope, he heard o' this,
> He thought it wouldna be amiss
> To hae a horse in readiness
> To flee awa' in the morning.
> Hey Johnny Cope, are ye waukin' yet?
> Or are your drums a-beatin' yet? . . .

Outside the cantonment there was no sign of trouble; the wide road, tree-flanked, stood empty but for the occasional sweeper, an industrious Untouchable keeping the cantonment's contiguous area clean for the sahibs and mem-sahibs of the Raj. Here and there a soldier, British or Indian, slammed to the halt and faced towards the marching men to salute the officer. The route into the town was lengthy; as Ogilvie began to approach the sleazy, shanty-like outskirts, he felt a difference in the air. Natives were gathering, staring in silence at what suddenly began to feel like an actual cortège, but a cortège whose principal actor was yet alive. From ahead came a body of native infantry under a *havildar;* as the escort passed by the native troops were fallen-out to chase the incipient mob away by the use of long, polished wooden staves. A murmur arose from the rear, and Ogilvie gave the order for the pipes and drums, silent once out of barracks, to start up again. The martial sound rose over that of the crowd's increasing hostility. Marching on, the escort came between more native troops, standing at ease at intervals to line the roadway with the mob massing behind their backs. In rear of the escort, Colour-Sergeant MacTrease marched stolidly along with his pace-stick under his arm, watching the step, and watching for trouble at the same time. Along the flank the section-sergeants marched, brushing past the soldiers lining the road, brushing past ragged natives, putting a hard face upon it but all the while half fearing the sudden slide of a knife, the blade that would kill before its owner, sinking back into the protective crowd, could be identified.

It was a situation in which those in rear and on the flanks, at any rate, felt a constant desire to cast looks over their shoulders. As the advance continued into the town the numbers of natives increased; the troops lining the roadway were having difficulty in containing them: Ogilvie began to sweat as the mob's murmurings grew and insults were hurled against the Raj, but, outwardly unruffled, he continued calmly with the escort, the pipes and drums beating out above the clamour and playing them in towards the civil jail now distantly in sight. As the marching men closed that distant prospect, the throwing of stones started: missiles, including all manner of filth, dropped upon the Scots. A heavy stone took Ogilvie on the left shoulder, causing him to stagger and momentarily lose the step. Recovering his balance, he kept his eyes front and carried on, ready on the instant to draw the revolver from the pouch at his belt if needs be. The clamour from the mob grew louder: in the rear file a man fell out with blood streaming from a jagged cut above the left eye, inflicted by a hard-flung stone. At once Colour-Sergeant MacTrease detached two men to his assistance and the escort carried on with the wounded private held safe on either side. On MacTrease's order, a corporal fell out and doubled up the line of advance to report to Ogilvie.

"Blood's been drawn, sir. A man cut by a stone."

"Thank you, Corporal MacKay."

"They'll be drawn to the blood, sir, like sharks in the sea."

"You've too much imagination, MacKay. Fall in and carry on."

"Aye, sir." The NCO doubled back again, eyes darting everywhere. Ahead of Ogilvie, the two pipers and the drummers were doing their best to drown the menacing sounds from the crowd. In the centre of the escort Sudak Khan was looking about him as though seeking his opportunity to take advantage of the situation if and when his compatriots broke through the Scots ranks. But the men on either side of him were close; and in his immediate rear the sergeant in charge of the personal escort, sweating like a pig now, was ready to use his bayonet if he had to. The head of the column was within some half-mile of the jail when the boil burst: a hundred yards ahead of the pipes and drums the mob swelled out from the sides of the road, bursting through the lining troops from both sides to converge in the roadway, yelling, casting their missiles, brandishing sticks and the odd snaky-bayoneted *jezail* reminiscent of the Frontier, all set for a determined blocking of the British advance. The press of bodies seemed to extend all the way back to the jail itself, solidly filling the road.

At once, Ogilvie halted the escort; the pipes and drums fell silent. From the rear, Colour-Sergeant MacTrease doubled up for orders.

"Form square, Colour MacTrease. Prisoner in the centre. All ranks to kneel."

"Aye, sir." MacTrease winced as a chunk of earth broke on his chest; fury showed in his face. "Do we open fire, sir?"

"You'll wait for my order, Colour MacTrease."

"Aye, sir. I trust it'll not be long in coming, sir. Those buggers—"

Ogilvie cut him short. "Form square, and quickly."

MacTrease gave a butt salute and turned about. Moving fast, he called the orders as the missiles continued coming across from both sides. The Scots re-formed in square, the men kneeling in the roadway with their rifles facing outwards. Sudak Khan was forced down in the centre, his arms held fast. Ogilvie and his subalterns stood, faces grim, uniforms spattered with filth, blood running from skin torn and grazed by the stones. When a movement towards the square seemed imminent, Ogilvie addressed the yelling natives in English: his Pushtu would most probably not be understood by the Southern Indians.

"Keep your distance or I open fire!"

He shouted the words, but his voice was lost in the over-all din. Then he saw MacTrease getting to his feet and pointing towards the jail, and calling out something he was not able to catch. He turned and looked to the front of his intended advance: the mass of natives was on the move now, surging down upon the Scots. He passed the order to MacTrease, who had now approached within earshot: "Front and flanks, fire over their heads, one volley only."

MacTrease yelled the order in his best parade-ground voice. The rifles came up, elevated just above the heads of the mob, and were discharged in a ripple of flame and smoke. There was some lessening of the mob noise and the nearer natives pressed back until they were stopped by those behind. MacTrease could be heard saying something about a bloody rabble who'd more than asked for a bullet in the gut; as the gunsmoke died away, blown by a light breeze, the clamour increased again. The mob ahead had halted some thirty yards off: this was perhaps progress of a sort. By this time Lord Brora, Ogilvie thought, would undoubtedly have fired into the mass; but what would have been the result? The answer to that must now be the responsibility of the

41

officer on the spot—himself; and it had two tongues. Either the order, once given, could win the day, or it could precipitate an attack in which the vastly outnumbered Scots, never mind the casualties that would be inflicted on the natives, must be overwhelmed unless assistance arrived in time. That could not now arrive before heavy losses had been sustained by his company. So much was clear.

Ogilvie found MacTrease at his side, breathing hard, eyes wide with anger. "Will you give the order now, sir, please?"

"Not yet, Colour."

"The Colonel—"

"The Colonel's not here. You have my decision. There's been no attack as such yet, and the prisoner's secure."

"We'll never get through, Captain Ogilvie. We'll not have a hope in hell!"

Ogilvie dashed the sweat from his face, saw blood on his hand when it came away, though he had not been conscious of being struck again. A moment later there was another and more positive movement from the mob to the left of the roadway, a press of men was pushed forward from behind, urged towards the British square in a heap of gesticulating, stick-waving, maddened, would-be killers. Now Ogilvie knew he could wait no longer, that this must be considered the attack. He swung round on MacTrease and was about to give the order to open fire point-blank into the seething native mass when a diversion came. The noise from the mob ahead had increased to a crescendo, but on a different note: a note now of something like fear, even panic. Ogilvie looked ahead. From the direction of the jail and visible over the heads of the mob, a solid phalanx of turbans was advancing briskly, rising and falling, and guidons were blowing in the breeze from the raised lances: the cavalry was coming in! As the mob streamed away to leave the road clear, a trumpet sounded and the squadron of horse, lowering its lance-points to catch and impale the stragglers, moved into a charge at the gallop. As the squadron split in two, half riding to the right and half to the left, more horsemen were seen in the centre, thundering down in a great cloud of dust, and the rattle of heavy equipment was heard, the unmistakable sound of guns and limber wheels. Ogilvie saw the frogged jackets of the gunners as they swept down; a cheer broke out spontaneously from the Scots as the horse artillery moved in. Ogilvie, catching the sardonic eye of Colour-Sergeant MacTrease, read the message: the cheers were certainly not for him.

Four

"I UNDERSTAND YOU handed over the prisoner."

"Yes, Colonel."

"And that by now he will have been despatched." Lord Brora, seated behind his desk, pulled out a gold half-hunter watch and studied it. "Yes. He will have swung, and good riddance. So you got him there, Captain Ogilvie. Praise be to God!" He looked Ogilvie up and down, his eyes bleak. "To God, and not to you. Reports have reached me from the Provost-Marshal."

"May I ask, Colonel— what reports?"

"You may ask and I shall answer," Brora said evenly, flicking a speck of dust from his uniformed sleeve. The sun streaming through the large window reflected gold-coloured gleams from his badges of rank. "A situation arose, it appears, one to which you failed to respond— to respond as ordered not an hour previously, Captain Ogilvie! What have you to say to that?"

Lord Brora's head was held back superciliously so that the eyes stared down-nose at Ogilvie, cold and hostile. Ogilvie, knowing very well that no answer would be acceptable to Lord Brora other than one that admitted the correctness of his own order, simply stated the facts as he had seen them at the time. He said, "I decided that to open fire would not be necessary, Colonel."

"Why?"

"The situation wasn't out of hand, Colonel."

"But was about to become so, I am told. Had you fired into that mob—"

"It would have instantly become an inflamed mob."

"Shut your mouth, sir! How dare you interrupt me!" Brora's eyes flashed fire. "I shall not tolerate impudence and insubordination in any of my officers, is that clear?"

"Yes, Colonel. I'm sorry."

Brora continued staring, but relaxed a little in his chair. "You are the son and heir of the Northern Army Commander—so much, of course, I'm well enough aware of. We in the regiment have much respect for Sir Iain. I advise you, however, not to play upon that."

Ogilvie flushed. "I would never do that, Colonel!"

"Well, we shall see. I am not impressed with you, Ogilvie, far from it. I dislike having my orders—if not disobeyed precisely—then treated with a certain cavalier disregard. If I thought you had treated them thus from some wish to avoid action, from cowardice perhaps, than I would break you whoever your father happened to be." Brora held up a hand as Ogilvie was about to interrupt. "Hold your tongue, young man, and hear me out. The cowardice I cannot prove, so shall say no more. The fact remains that you carried out your mission and the prisoner was safely delivered. But for that the thanks are to God as I have said, and to the charge of the Deccan Horse, who delivered you from your predicament. Do you deny that, Ogilvie?"

Ogilvie met his eyes straight. "I don't deny that, Colonel."

"Good! That shows a certain honesty at all events." Brora rose to his feet, tall and majestic. "Now I have only this to say, and you will heed and remember: you allowed your regiment—*my* regiment—to be damn well *rescued* by native cavalry! I detest the damn natives and I'm no lover of the damn cavalry either. Cavalrymen are *pimps* with insufferable airs and graces, stupid men of doubtful morals and no damn use once their horses have been shot away. Why, their damn boots alone are so heavy they can't move an inch in the field!" Brora's face was almost apoplectic, purple with massed blood; he seemed to have forgotten that his new GOC had been of the derided cavalry. "Today's escort was the first Southern Command has seen of the Royal

45

Strathspeys, Captain Ogilvie, and you managed to give 'em a damn rotten view of us! I'll find it hard to forgive that, but as a fair man I shall try. Now get out of my sight."

*　　　*　　　*

That afternoon regimental transport took James Ogilvie to Mettupalayam and the station for the climbing mountain train that would carry him into the Nilgiri Hills and the pleasant, cool atmosphere of Ootacamund and his call upon General Farrar-Drumm. He felt philosophic about Brora's tantrum, though still bloody-minded about the hint at cowardice. Brora was a man given to exaggeration and had to be accepted as such; his reign was, thankfully, not due to last, though he would continue as second-in-command once Lord Dornoch was fit for duty. Sitting in a corner of the carriage as the little engine chuffed and panted, pushing the short train out of Coimbatore, Ogilvie shrugged Brora out of his mind: amid the rewards of regimental life, it was inevitable there should be the occasional cross to bear. Without, he hoped, being guilty of the enervating sin of self-satisfaction, Ogilvie believed he had conducted the escort in a responsible manner: no lives had been lost as a result of his own actions and that was good. That there had been an element of luck was not to be denied, but then that could have been said of almost any military endeavour since the start of time . . .

The prospect from the train windows was a pleasing one. As the railway climbed into the hills, the physical face of India seemed to fade away along with the heat of the plains. The scenery consisted now of rolling hills, many of them forested but many of them not unlike the South Downs of Sussex; in the summer the Nilgiris would be a riot of colour—buttercups, harebells, blue gentian, anemones, dog-roses, wild orchids, strawberry flowers, clematis, pimpernel. With each foot of increased height above and to the north of Coimbatore, the temperature grew more tolerable. At this time of year it could be really cold in Ootacamund, as

46

Ogilvie knew, ice and frost not being at all unusual, with the latter each early morning bringing its brittle film to the proliferating flowers in the gardens of the British residents. Met at the mountain railhead by transport from Southern Army Headquarters, Ogilvie looked with interest at the sprawling hill station with its curiously mixed architecture, overwhelmingly English and in truth not particularly beautiful, many of the buildings, erected largely in the last thirty years, coloured a deep terra-cotta red. There was an occasional officer in uniform going about his duty, and there were many elderly gentlemen, clearly retired majors and colonels of the Indian Army, with their ladies on their arms; and there were the ubiquitous natives in saris or bundled into shawls against the cold of the Nilgiris, many of them silent and inert against the trunks of great eucalyptus trees, staring with bright eyes of black at the passing world. From a bandstand, just as though the scene were Eastbourne or Hove or Bournemouth or Tunbridge Wells, the orchestral instruments of a British regiment, the 2nd Middlesex, the 57th and 77th Foot, played a selection of light music to a seated audience and a number of leave-taking strollers enjoying the crisp cold before their eventual return to duty in hot Madras and other choresome centres of the governance of the Raj.

At Headquarters, after a smart turn-out by the gate guard, Ogilvie was taken in hand by a salaaming and resplendent major-domo and ceremoniously escorted to the apartments of the Major-General Commanding, Southern Army. Sir Clarence Farrar-Drumm, in full uniform except for his headgear, was reclining upon a *chaise-longue,* an early Victorian piece that seemed curiously appropriate both to Ootacamund and its military occupant.

When his visitor was announced, Sir Clarence swung his legs to the floor and with some difficulty and wheezing stood upright, seizing a stick during the manoeuvre and leaning his weight upon it until it bent and appeared in imminent danger of shattering.

"Ah, Ogilvie," he said.

"Sir!"

"That's right, isn't it—hey? I mean, you *are* young Ogilvie, are you not?"

"Yes, sir."

"Ah, good, I thought you were. Yes." Sir Clarence cleared his throat of rumbling phlegm, and, lifting his stick, waved it towards a wide window behind him. There was a splendid view of the enclosing hills. "Familiar, my boy?"

"I beg your pardon, sir?"

"Like Scotland— doncher think?"

"Yes, indeed, sir."

"Yes, well. I dessay you like it but I must confess I don't. Scotland I mean. *Awful* country to be frank— I'm sorry if I sound rude, don't mean to be, just speak the truth that's all. Got no damn cavalry, of course—except the Greys. If you say *they're* civilised, I'll agree with you. What?"

"Yes, sir."

Farrar-Drumm lifted his stick and aimed it at Ogilvie. "That's all you've uttered so far— yes, sir. Not very original, that. Sit down. Over there, my boy, where I'm pointing."

The stick was in fact still pointing straight at Ogilvie; using the initiative which he guessed the General would equate with originality, he turned about. Sure enough, there was a chair. He sat; Farrar-Drumm moved towards him, remaining standing.

"Need to stand a while each day," the General said. "If I don't, the damn bones set, doncher know. Touch of rheumatics according to the damn leech."

"I'm sorry to hear that, sir," Ogilvie said politely.

"Oh, don't be, don't be. I shall live." Farrar-Drumm's face between the heavy white whiskers was as red as a beetroot, possible due to the potent bottled agency by which life was retained in his shaky body. "How's yer father, hey?"

"Well, as I believe, sir. It's some time since I've seen my parents."

48

"Yes, yes, that's Ogilvie as I recall him—no damn favouritism towards a son. Very right and proper, of course—I admire him for it. Yer mother's a damn fine woman, too. First-class rider to hounds—for a woman. Whom does she hunt with now—the Peshawar Vale?"

Ogilvie coughed in some embarrassment; generals seldom liked being corrected, but there was no escape. "My mother doesn't hunt, sir, as a matter of fact—"

"Not hunt, not hunt?" White eyebrows lifted. "Well, I'll be damned! Must be thinking of someone else, but never mind." The General was seized by a fit of coughing. *"Chota-peg?"* he asked when it subsided.

"Well, sir—"

"Thought you would. Clap your hands, if you please, young Ogilvie."

Ogilvie did so; the doors were flung open and a turbaned native appeared and salaamed. Farrar-Drumm said, *"Chota-pegs* for the Captain sahib and myself."

"At once, General sahib." The native bowed himself out and Farrar-Drumm made at last towards a chair, a hard upright one onto which he dropped somewhat heavily. The native bearer, returning with the whisky on a silver salver with a siphon, brought small, elegant walnut tables to set beside each officer's chair. A toast was perfunctorily drunk and Farrar-Drumm sank half his *chota-peg* and looked immediately grateful for it. After this he became discursive, not to say garrulous; he talked of Scotland, appearing to forget his earlier comment upon the country. He talked of Sir Iain Ogilvie, of that officer's long family connection with the regiment, of his fine record in peace and war, of the honour of the Ogilvies of Corriecraig and of the 114th Highlanders. Finally, after some fifteen minutes of monologue, he barked at Ogilvie: "What's your ambition, hey?"

"To command the battalion, sir."

"A good ambition. I'm pleased with your answer. But have you no hankering for the staff?"

49

"Not a hankering, sir. I prefer regimental soldiering. But I realise that eventual promotion requires staff experience first."

"Yes. So in fact your ambitions go beyond command of the battalion?"

"Not really, sir. I'd be satisfied with that."

The General clicked his tongue. "An officer should never be satisfied, my dear boy, especially a young one. But time may change your views, and your ambition will grow with rank. It's a great thing, doncher know, to be one of Her Majesty's General Officers."

"Yes, sir."

"A matter for much pride. Yer father would agree. Talking of yer father, another chance of great honour is about to come the way of yet another Ogilvie." Farrar-Drumm sounded somewhat mysterious; he went on, "I refer to you, my boy."

"Me, sir?"

"Yes. That is one of the reasons I sent for you. Yer Colonel will by now have been apprised of the orders for his battalion, and you are about to learn them yourself. They are as follows: the 114th Highlanders are ordered to join the camp of exercise, as it is called, entraining on Monday of next week for Secunderabad. With you will go the rest of your new brigade—the Border Regiment and the Madras Light Infantry. All three will act as stiffeners, to give, from their Frontier experience, a harder air of reality to my own command than has been possible for some years. If you are not as yet familiar with camps of exercise, you will become so. I shall send a staff officer to brief all officers of your brigade before you entrain." Farrar-Drumm paused. "I have sent for you, my boy, because I have special orders, and a very special and important mission, for you in particular . . ."

*   *   *

General Farrar-Drumm might well have been, once, the strong disciplinarian that Lord Brora had said he was: but

50

now he had been mellowed by age. He had addressed Ogilvie in almost avuncular terms and had once again been garrulous about the Ogilvie family honour and inherited military background. It took him a little while to get to the point which, when baldly stated, was simple enough: staying with him as his honoured guest in Ootacamund was a personage from a Royal house, Prince George of Hohenzollern, German son of a sister of King Oscar of Sweden. The visit was strictly unofficial and there was no entourage beyond a personal man-servant. Prince George, a young man of military background himself, had expressed a wish to acquire some experience of the British Army; and Sir Clarence had made the suggestion, most eagerly accepted, that the Prince should accompany the brigade to the camp of exercise at Secunderabad.

"His Royal Highness," Sir Clarence observed, "will then see how men from the North-West Frontier, accustomed to forays and patrols and battles, conduct themselves. A salutary experience, I believe."

"Yes, sir."

"And now to your part in my plan. With the approval of yer Colonel—yet to be obtained, I should add—His Royal Highness will be placed in your personal charge and care, to be shewn everything that a young officer should be shewn, to take such part in the activities of the regiment as he may wish, and—above all, Ogilvie—to be protected and kept safe from harm so that in due course he may return to his own country safe, sound and wholesome." Further explanation established that the use of the word "wholesome" was due to certain youthful exuberances on the part of His Royal Highness; freed from the heavy restrictions of the provincial German court where his ducal father held sway, the Prince's eye had roved over-eagerly towards the younger wives and daughters of the British officers of Ootacamund. "His Royal Highness the Duke would *not* approve," Sir Clarence said sombrely. "The Prince must be shewn how to pursue other interests. Needs exercise, that's what—tire his body,

51

doncher know— walking, riding, hunting, shooting, that sort of thing. The camp of exercise is just what's called for." The General wagged a solemn finger. "I'm relying upon you, Ogilvie. It is a high responsibility. I know you will discharge it worthily."

*   *   *

"Worthily" was an all-embracing word, as solemn as the wagging of the General's finger: Ogilvie, at his first meeting with Prince George of Hohenzollern, doubted the long continuance of dull worthiness. His Royal Highness was an exceedingly pleasant young man, not in the least stuffy as his German-Swedish royal parentage might have suggested. He had laughter in his face and in his eyes; he was tall and strongly built and though only nineteen was well able to hold his own in conversation at the General's dinner table that night. He was not, as might have been expected, overawed by age, yet neither was he in the least overweening or brash. Of royal birth, he had royal manners and much charm also. Ogilvie took an immediate liking to him, and found to his relief that the Prince spoke excellent English beneath the guttural sounds of his German accent. He looked as though he had the makings of a first-class soldier, yet there was something about his polite attentiveness to the General's elderly lady that suggested he was also the womaniser of Sir Clarence's scarlet fears. And if that were the case, then so were any number of excellent soldiers, Ogilvie's own father among them. After dinner Sir Clarence and Lady Farrar-Drumm retired early to bed and the Prince and Ogilvie were left with the brandy and the General's ADC. The Prince's face grew flushed and his eyes merrier, and he remarked that much as he was enjoying his stay with the General he found certain deficiencies in Ootacamund.

Ogilvie asked cautiously, "What sort of deficiencies, sir?"

"Sir?" The Prince frowned, then gave a boisterous laugh. "All the time at dinner you have addressed me as Your Royal

Highness or as Sir. I do not wish this if we are to serve together in your regiment. Tell me, please: you are an English gentleman, are you not?"

"Not," Ogilvie said, catching the eye of the ADC and giving a barely perceptible wink. "Scottish!"

The Prince inclined his head; the gilded star of a Swedish order scraped against his starched shirt-front. "I am so sorry. You will accept my apology? But as a Scottish gentleman, there is no difference between us. I am George, you are James, if you will permit?"

Ogilvie laughed gladly. "Of course I permit as you put it. Now, the deficiencies?"

"I think you understand very well," the Prince answered. "In my country it is the same—in both my countries! Always the chaperon. It is so . . . so stultifying. A man needs his diversions, is this not so?"

"Indeed it's so." Ogilvie gave a cough of some slight embarrassment: chaperons stood as formidably against British officers as they did against German princes, and there had been a good deal of factual wisdom in the General's earlier words about riding and so on. Gratification was not easily come by in India: as at home one did not seduce young ladies of gentle birth, but unlike home there were no others available apart from the native women, and to bed with them was in most cases the prerogative of officers too elderly and unattractive to charm white women . . . and yawning gaps arose in many an officer's foreign-service life unless he was lucky enough to find a pretty widow.

Prince George waved a hand. "It is no matter for now. I find your company very excellent, gentlemen. But perhaps in Coimbatore, when I join your regiment, James—perhaps then there will be the escapade, no?"

It was the ADC who answered the question, smilingly. "There's little scope in Coimbatore, I fear. It's a dreary place outside cantonments. If it's life you want, you must visit Madras!"

"Which won't be yet," Ogilvie said. "My regiment's

bound for Secunderabad, as you know."

"Yes, and I am eager to go there." The Prince refilled his brandy glass. "Let us drink to much fun and happiness in Secunderabad, James." He lifted the glass: his hands, Ogilvie noticed, were big, heavy. Capable horseman's hands . . . but they gripped the stem a shade too tightly. The fine glass broke, the brandy poured down mixed with blood from the Prince's palm. Naturally, they all made light of it; but afterwards Ogilvie was to wonder if it had been a premonition.

*　　*　　*

Next day Ogilvie returned alone to Coimbatore, riding down from the Nilgiri Hills in the little chuffing mountain train, down into the close heat of the plains again, the heat, the sweat and the dust of workaday military life. With him he carried a letter personally addressed from Sir Clarence to Lord Brora; and this he handed to the Adjutant who promised early delivery.

Within the hour Ogilvie was sent for to the Colonel's quarters.

"Ah, Captain Ogilvie." Brora was in fact sitting in his bath tub, an attentive bearer at his side pouring warm water like a human fountain to remove soap from his Colonel sahib. "That letter from the General. Your doing?"

"Not my doing, Colonel, though of course I accepted the General's wishes."

Brora grinned. "No damn option, had you? Wishes my arse! It was an order and you know it." He heaved his body more upright against the bath tub's metal back; thick hair showed, covering chest and stomach like a mat. "Bloody nuisance. This is a battalion of infantry, not a damn kindergarten—which is an appropriate enough word! I dislike the whole blasted German race, frankly. However I, like you, am the recipient of an order so there's no more to be said. Except this, Ogilvie: I'm not to be bothered with

54

him. He's yours, all yours. See you take charge of him and don't let him interfere with my regimental efficiency or you'll be the one to suffer. And see he's kept *safe*—that seems to be important to Sir Clarence. Understood?"

"Yes, Colonel."

"And there seems to be some sort of attendant, a valet. The Prince is not exactly visiting incognito, but he hasn't brought any ADCs or whatever—just this valet feller by the name of Knicken. Well, Knicken'll have to be wished onto the Sergeants' Mess, I suppose."

"Yes, Colonel."

"Right! Off you go, then." Suddenly, Brora gave a shout of rage and turned upon the bearer. "God damn you, don't stand there doing nothing! *Pour water,* you God-forsaken damn heathen."

"Yes, sahib. Pour, sahib. Water, sahib. A hundred thousand apologies, sahib."

Ogilvie, who disliked terrified cringing, turned away. As he left the Colonel's bungalow, he heard Brora's voice continuing its tirade. At dinner that night, neither Brora nor Black were in the Mess; it seemed they had been bidden to dine with Brigadier-General Masefield at Brigade. The atmosphere was more pleasant than for many days past, and after dinner there was some noisy tomfoolery from the subalterns, who turned the ante-room upside down as they shifted heavy furniture to make into jumps for human horses and riders, an exercise that in the past had sometimes led to broken arms and legs and was much frowned on by Surgeon Major Corton. Corton, trying now to read a newspaper from home, ancient enough in all conscience, sighed and glanced at Ogilvie.

"Use your authority, James, for God's sake!"

Ogilvie grinned. "Let's put up with it, shall we? We've all suffered enough recently!"

"Then why suffer more?" Corton sighed again, then returned Ogilvie's grin. "Oh, well, they're only young once and I dare say steam has to be let off, but why it has to be let off around me I really don't know." He went back to his newspaper, called through the mêlée to a Mess waiter for brandy, and lit a cigar. The noise went on; a chair fell by the wayside, one of its legs broken. Nothing seemed to dampen the subalterns' spirits; nothing, that was, until a furious voice, lifted in a shout, stopped everything dead.

"What the devil's going on there, damn you all to hell!"

In the doorway Lord Brora stood, Andrew Black looking disapproving at his side. "Captain Ogilvie!"

"Colonel?'

"Have you taken leave of your senses, Captain Ogilvie? What possessed you to permit the smashing up of the entire ante-room?"

"I'm sorry, Colonel. In fact there's been little damage, only a chair—"

"Don't you damn well argue with me, Captain Ogilvie, I am *right*. The chair will be paid for by the members of the Mess responsible, as will any other damage. You will all kindly go to your beds, gentlemen—and I shall see *you* in the morning, Captain Ogilvie. This is most scandalous behaviour with the battalion about to move out of cantonments into the field!" With Black, Lord Brora turned on his heel and left the ante-room. Ogilvie seethed. A colonel who treated his officers as a nanny might treat her charges would not prove one to inspire confidence if the movement into the field on exercises should turn out to lead to action. Ogilvie spent that night largely in indignant sleeplessness; when morning came he had a throbbing headache and a feeling of disinclination to get out of bed. After breakfast a summons came for all officers to attend upon the Colonel in the ante-room, now restored to its proper dignity. No reference was made at the assembly to the night before: it seemed to have passed from Brora's mind—but upon that mind, apparently, much else sat heavily, not the least weighty matter being that of His Royal Highness Prince George of Hohenzollern.

"We have a damn foreigner being attached for his blasted

amusement, gentlemen. A German of all things, no doubt here to learn British secrets and pass them on to the damn German Emperor so he can the better make war upon us at his convenience. The one thing in his favour is that he's not a damn Russian." Briefly Brora explained the circumstances. "I want you know, to be in no damn doubt, that this princeling is Captain Ogilvie's responsibility, no one else's. It's between him and Sir Clarence Farrar-Drumm, for whom until now I've always had the greatest respect. For ears outside this room, I still have— bear that in mind at your peril otherwise, gentlemen. Now to more important things. Captain Black?"

"Ready, Colonel." Black cleared his throat, leapt to his feet, and took Brora's place, a sheaf of documents in his hand. "I have the orders for the camp of exercise inside the state of Hyderabad . . ." The Adjutant's harsh voice laid down the framework; after arrival at Secunderabad, they and other units were to be exercised in attack upon mock native caravans containing contraband arms; there would be attacks by troops acting as "natives" upon British road convoys who for their part would show their mettle in defence; there would be night forays, patrols into "enemy" territory, and outpost duties. The reality of it was all too familiar to the Scots. Taking part would be, in addition to Masefield's brigade, large formations of infantry and cavalry with their attached horse and field artillery, these troops being already in the area of Secunderabad. The manoeuvres would clearly be on a large scale; and Black added a warning.

"You'll recall what was said before we entrained from Peshawar: there's trouble brewing along the southern border of the state of Hyderabad. We now have word that the leader of the possible revolt— the Rajah of Rangapore— is massing men of his private army between the Tunga Bhadra and the Kistna Rivers. That is well south of Secunderabad, of course, but we shall, if asked, be ready to give immediate assistance to the Nizam."

Five

MORE INSPECTIONS, MORE parades, more train journeys; and then, not into a new cantonment, but into camp south-west of Secunderabad for a night's stay before marching into the exercise area. During the journey north into the Nizam's dominions, Ogilvie had come to know Prince George of Hohenzollern a good deal better and had been reinforced in his liking of the young German, who had accepted the discomforts of the rattling train cheerfully. With the man-servant Klaus Knicken, Prince George had joined the regiment in cantonments a couple of days after Lord Brora's acceptance of his temporary attachment had been notified to Sir Clarence in Ootacamund. Even Brora had seemed to some extent charmed and mollified by the Prince's manner. Ogilvie himself had made the introduction in the Mess, and Prince George had clicked his heels together and bowed from the waist.

"My lord. I am most grateful to you."

"Sir will do," Brora had said shortly. "I trust you'll enjoy your stay. If there is anything you need, ask Captain Ogilvie."

"I shall, sir. Thank you again. You are most kind."

"Remember you're attached as a visitor, as a guest. Not as a combatant officer. I understand you have the equivalent rank of second lieutenant in the German Army?"

"I have, sir—"

"Your fiat does not run within my regiment, and of course you'll not wear your uniform. Otherwise you are welcome and free to do as you please."

58

Prince George bowed again. "I am most grateful, sir. But I would wish to place myself under your orders as my Colonel."

"You would, would you?" Lord Brora stared the German up and down for a moment, rising and falling on the balls of his feet with his hands behind his immense back. "Then you'll have to find yourself another wish, Prince. I am sorry I cannot accommodate you, but the matter rests precisely as I've already indicated." He snapped his fingers for the Mess waiter. "*Chota-pegs* for the Prince and myself. Prince, we shall drink two toasts: Her Majesty the Queen-Empress, and her grandson the Emperor of Germany." Somewhat enigmatically Brora had added, half to himself, "May they always live at peace." The toasts had been duly drunk when the whisky came; afterwards Ogilvie had reflected that to his knowledge it had been the first time the Colonel had bought anyone a drink in the Mess. Thereafter Brora had been immensely civil to the Prince each time their paths had crossed. During the few days before entraining Prince George had been Ogilvie's constant companion, taking an interest in everything that he was shewn and told, and talking in a friendly way to the NCOs and men who, it was obvious, liked him as much as Ogilvie did. The Regimental Sergeant-Major seemed especially impressed.

"A very worthwhile young gentleman, Captain Ogilvie. Soldierly and smart, and his face shows spirit. What would his regiment be, sir, do you know?"

"Uhlan Guards, Sarn't Major. Prussian light cavalry—lancers." Ogilvie hid a grin as he went on, "He's intrigued by the bagpipes. He'd like to know how they're constructed."

"I'll have a word with Pipe-Major Ross, sir."

Ogilvie laid a hand on Cunningham's shoulder. "Don't take me too literally, Bosom. He wonders if they're alive or dead. But he likes the sound they make!"

"So I should hope, Captain Ogilvie, sir, so I should hope indeed." Cunningham's tone was prim. "Will there be anything else, sir?"

*   *   *

The battalion lines, with exact spaces between tents minutely measured under Cunningham's all-seeing eye, shone white and clean as the sun went down the sky and Sunset, sounding out on the strident bugles, played the Union Flag down the flagstaff before the presented arms of the guard, the slings of their rifles shining whiter than the tents, as white as the pipeclayed belts worn for guard duty in replacement of the leather that would be worn normally in camp and in the field. Later, after Last Post when the light had left the sky and the fingers of the night had crept out across the lines, Ogilvie stood and listened, as he had so often listened, to the solitary strains coming from Pipe-Major Ross as he played the regiment to bed on his pipes. The notes were strangely sad, haunting as the playing of a solitary piper always contrived to be. Turning away when the tune had faded, Ogilvie found Prince George standing silent behind him, a cigar glowing in his fingers.

"That was impressive, James. Out here in the wide open . . . you understand what I mean, I think?"

"Yes, I do. I'm glad you found it impressive." Ogilvie gave a short laugh touched with embarrassment. "I find it hard to put my own feelings into words."

"I understand that also, James." Prince George drew on his cigar for a moment. "In Germany, it is true, we are more inclined than are you English to talk of our patriotism and our pride in our army— our soldiers and our officer corps. Yet this I myself find difficult— I do not know why." He paused. "It is perhaps because I am half Swedish— I cannot say."

Ogilvie grinned in the darkness. "Does it worry you, George?"

"I think it does, yes." There was a longish pause before the young German went on with some diffidence and hesitancy. "I find it a fault in myself, I think. So many of our generals and field-marshals are men of vigorous speech,

60

boastful— men largely of the stamp of von Bismarck, a most terrible person." The Prince seemed to catch his breath. "A personal view only, and expressed to you impulsively, as my friend. It will not be repeated?"

"Of course it won't! Shall we go back to the lines?" Ogilvie had strolled beyond the end of his company lines, towards the guarded perimeter where, had they been still on the Frontier, a protective ditch would have been dug and a rampart thrown up against tribal forays. Now he turned with the Prince and walked slowly back through the darkness towards the rows of tents with their sleeping soldiers inside. The Prince, seeming to seek company and not to wish to turn in yet, spoke again, in a low voice, sombrely.

"I am perhaps not a soldier, James, in my heart. I have not yet found that out. All I have known is the ceremonial, the pomp and the display, the marching and the bands. I do not know yet how I shall face the reality."

"Action?"

The Prince nodded. "You have been in action. What is it like, when the glory is taken away?"

Ogilvie didn't answer at once; the question had been seriously asked and must be seriously answered. The Prince would want the truth and would see through pretence: he had asked the question perhaps because he had already seen through pretence, through the shallow veneer of those who said that soldiers were never afraid. Many times, Ogilvie had been afraid; so scared before an action that his hands had gone white and had shaken as if with the palsy . . . He said, "For our own sakes, we mustn't take all the glory away. It's that that keeps us all going! That's why we have the Colours— that's why we have the pipes. If there were no thoughts of glory, half the chaps wouldn't move when the order came. At least, not till they were driven."

"Driven by what, James?"

Ogilvie gave a short laugh. "Why, by the sergeants and corporals, in the case of the men!"

"And in the case of the officers?"

Another laugh, a harder one. "By thoughts of glory and duty—which are not unknown to the rank and file as well, of course. Or by something else."

"Yes?"

"The fear of fear. The fear of being branded."

"As a coward?"

Ogilvie nodded.

"They are afraid, your British officers and men?"

"Frequently! I would go further and say they're always afraid before action starts—all of them. We would have to be very stupid not to be. Once it starts, it's different. You forget fear because there's so much else to think about. You're on the move, or you're firing, or you're looking for cover, and you have other people to think about as well as yourself. You have responsibilities."

"That is when glory takes over?"

Ogilvie grinned. "Yes, perhaps it is. Don't brood too much, my dear chap. When the time comes—as one day it may—you'll be all right!"

"That's what von Bismarck has told me."

"That you'll be all right?"

"No. Such a matter I would not raise with von Bismarck—simply to speak of it, to have any doubts, would be frowned upon in Germany. Von Bismarck told me that one day the time would come. He foresees a war against the British Empire, and—" Suddenly the Prince broke off, and his body stiffened in the darkness. "I should not speak of these matters. It is both wrong and impolite. I am sorry. You will excuse me, James." Before Ogilvie could utter he had turned and was walking away, moving fast, going towards the tent set up for him by Ogilvie's bearer in the officers' lines. Ogilvie sauntered on behind, sniffing the cool night air, thinking about the young Prince and his anxieties. He smiled to himself about von Bismarck's prognostications. The ex-Chancellor of Germany, a very old gentleman now, had always been a fire-eater, iron willed and as hard as nails; but he had met his match when back in '88 Kaiser Wilhelm II had ascended the throne of the German Empire. The imperious man with the withered arm and the upturned moustache had proved no friend to von Bismarck, and warlike and ambitious as he undoubtedly was himself, he would be unlikely to accede to von Bismarck's desire to lift arms in anger against his equally imperious grandmother in Windsor Castle. Von Bismarck could be left to his restless and unwelcome retirement; Prince George of Hohenzollern was a more pressing worry. That young man seemed filled with self-doubt despite the soldierly bearing that had impressed the RSM, and Ogilvie was more than sorry that such was the case. At an equivalent age he, too, had had his doubts, but in his case there had been no considerations of princely status to make the issues worse. It took little enough imagination to appreciate the various pressures upon a basically unwarrior-like prince within the iron confines of the German Empire and the German court!

*   *   *

Next morning as the bugles blew Reveille the shouts of the NCOs could be heard even before the last notes had died away: the orders had already been passed for an early march, the commencement of the combined exercises. The officers of the brigade had been briefed by Masefield after dinner the previous night, all of them assembling at the large tent that housed Brigade Headquarters. Masefield's brigade was to be split up once they had left the encampment, each of the three regiments forming the nucleus of new formations that would be completed by Indian Army battalions attached to learn all they could from the battle-tried soldiers of Northern Command. The Royal Strathspey would remain under Masefield in his new brigade; and all three formations were to march on different and widely spaced routes south-westerly towards the Kistna River. The march was expected to be a long and hard one, with the nights passed in bivouacs, and en route the various exercises as outlined in the general orders notified in Ootacamund would be conducted, with Masefield's brigade playing the part of a stores and ammunition column susceptible to attack by supposed bandits, who would be supplied by sepoys of the private army of the Nizam of Hyderabad. At a date yet to be determined all three groups would come together again, with additional troops including cavalry, for the main part of the combined manoeuvres. Lord Brora expected a high standard throughout. He spoke to the whole battalion when camp had been struck and the tents packed neatly away in the commissariat wagons and on the backs of the transport mules and camels.

"You'll remember you're the 114th Highlanders," he said in his carrying voice. Slapping the flanks of his trews with his riding-crop he sat his horse facing the ranks. "An example to the native units that'll be joining us shortly, that's what I require you to be—every man! No slacking, no damn grumbling, no dropping out, although it's my intention to push the battalion to the limit. Captain Black?"

"Sir!" From horseback, the Adjutant saluted smartly.

"Any man that falls out, his name's to be taken and he's to be put on a charge."

"Sir!"

Lord Brora's voice grew even louder. "I am not a merciful man, thanks be to God. When on the march, at exercise or in action—and remember action's always a possibility in India—I show no mercy at all. I trust that is clear. I shall not repeat it, but you have all been warned. Captain Black?"

"Sir!"

"Carry on, if you please. The battalion to advance in column of route."

Again Black saluted and swung his horse round. He was brought up short by further words, loudly uttered, from the Colonel. "That prince. Where the devil is he?"

Looking flustered as he heard the shout, Prince George

64

was seen to scramble down from a commissariat wagon. He ran across towards Lord Brora and halted before his horse, standing rigidly at attention. "You wish me, sir?"

"Yes, by God! So you intend to ride as an old gentleman, do you, Prince, a passenger in a damn commissariat cart?"

"With your permission only, sir."

Brora stroked his chin, eyes flashing. "H'mmm. Well, so be it, then. I don't want damn civilian-dressed persons marching with my battalion, to be sure I don't! On the other hand . . ." He hesitated. "You look *untidy* in a wagon. Captain Black?"

"Sir!"

"A horse for His Royal Highness." Brora turned back to the Prince. "You'll ride with the damn Padre. Then you won't look odd. Your man can remain in the wagon, provided he keeps out of sight." His piercing gaze seemed to cut a trail through the early-morning air to where the Padre sat his horse, clad in a tail-coat of heavy black cloth, and wearing a black hat with a wide brim. "You could scarcely look odder," Brora said loudly and insultingly to the Prince, "than your companion-to-be. And now to horse, if you please."

He waited impatiently as the Prince's mount was brought up and the young man swung himself nimbly into the saddle. As he rode away, Brora's eyes followed him grudgingly: as befitted a cavalry officer of the Uhlans, the Prince's horsemanship was perfect. As prince and parson manoeuvred alongside each other behind the rearmost company but ahead of the commissariat train, the Colonel once again told Black to carry on. The Royal Strathspeys were turned left into column of route with rifles sloped, and in the lead ahead of the Colonel the pipes and drums beat out strongly, giving the step to the strains of "The 79th's Farewell to Gibraltar." From right and left the Border Regiment and the Madras Light Infantry wheeled in, the former taking the lead of the long column to the fifes and drums beating out "D'ye Ken John Peel", the men from Cumberland and Westmorland marching proudly and as smartly as if they had been on parade at the depot in Carlisle Castle. In front rode the Brigadier-General with his Brigade Major and orderly officer. As the sun climbed the metallic blue sky the heat increased and the clouds of dust raised by the marching feet settled upon men's sweat and turned it to a kind of mud: at any time of the year the central Indian plain with its Savanna-type climate was a terrible arena for a march. About a couple of miles from their late camp the brigade was met by the other two groups to make a splendid and immensely colourful assembly of force. The formations split to the orders of the Brigadier-General of the 114th's brigade, and the Borderers and the Madras Light Infantry wheeled away again into their new brigades and were replaced by the native units. When the transfer had been completed the bugles blew and Brigadier-General Masefield led out with the Royal Strathspeys, the 101st Royal Bengal Fusiliers and the 109th Bombay Infantry with their attached field artillery. As usual, Black was everywhere within his regimental column, riding up and down the Scots' line, dark face watchful for any signs of slackness, for rifles not held at the correct angle of slope, for unpolished buttons, badges and bayonet-scabbards, for any unsmart sag in the leather straps of the Slade-Wallace equipment that carried the water-bottles and the other impedimenta of infantry on the march. But after a while the ground was cut from under Black's feet: word was passed down from Brigade in the van that the column was to march at ease. Black's mouth thinned as collar-bands were loosened and rifles shifted from the slope to hang from shoulders by their slings, as the Wolseley helmets were eased from sweating brows and voices were raised in song. He touched spurs to his horse and trotted up the line to resume his place beside Lord Brora, back turned disdainfully to the troops. Brora seemed to sense his Adjutant's displeasure and commented upon it.

"You look unhappy, my dear fellow."

"Yes. I confess I feel it." There was a snap in Black's

voice. "I do not consider it good for the men to be indulged. Smartness is important, sir."

Brora glanced sideways again. "I think you have a fetish for detail, Black." Brora, as had been noticed by all the officers, disdained the regimental tradition for Christian names in informal conversation: and oddly, though he had issued no directive on the subject, Black himself had fallen into the habit of addressing the acting Colonel as "sir" more often than not. Whereas Lord Dornoch had always insisted on the regimental custom of being addressed as "Colonel" by his officers on all occasions both formal and informal, Brora had accepted the "sir" without comment and had in any case made it plain from the start that he was not to be addressed as "Major". Now, Brora went on, "We are not in cantonments, nor on formal parade. Smartness has its place — its vital place, indeed. I happen to agree with the Brigadier-General, a march such as ours is not necessarily that place."

"I do *not* agree, sir. The men are apt to misconstrue indulgence for weakness."

"Rubbish," Brora said briskly. "Not when it's properly applied. It's not indulgence, it's common sense. Why soak up energy when the fight is yet to come?"

Black shrugged. "Well, sir, if that's your view—"

"It is! Now save your own energy, my dear fellow, and let us consider our orders." Brora jerked his leather map case from its holder in front of his saddle and withdrew a rolled up map which, riding on as he did so, he unrolled and scanned. "Any time from *there*," he said, jabbing a finger down on some low hills ahead of the line of march, "we can expect the first exercise assault. There'll be others in the hills, but after that, once we're right into the plains, the attacks will come by night, and by night only in my opinion. The damn Deccan's too wide open for day attack."

"Other than in force, sir, yes."

Brora laughed. "It'd have to be a damn strong force!"

"The revolt is said to be well supported."

"The revolt, eh?" Brora seemed surprised at first, then nodded. "I take your point, Black, but I was not thinking of the revolt. Even if it does materialise, it won't be till we're much nearer the Kistna River."

"Perhaps . . ."

"And I doubt if they'd mount an attack on us. It's the bloody Nizam they're after!"

"Whom we support, sir."

"True." Once again Lord Brora glanced sideways. "Do you have a feeling, then, that trouble's on the way?"

"This is India," Black answered dourly.

"But not the Frontier. Perhaps you've been too long on the Frontier, Black, and it's filled your bonnet with buzzing bees!"

With a touch of anger Black responded, "Colonel, you yourself said, when speaking to the men—"

"Yes, yes, I know quite well what I said, thank you, Black." Brora laughed; not a pleasant laugh. "Propaganda! All soldiers are the better for the fear of God. Still, there was truth in it, I'll agree. And you may be right after all. So full vigilance, Black. You may impress that on the officers and NCOs at the next fall-out."

"Very good, sir. When do you suppose that will be ordered, may I ask?"

"When Masefield so decides, I expect," Brora answered disagreeably, "but I intend to suggest to him that it shall not be yet. I have set my mind upon physical and mental alertness. The men are to be driven hard today and for many days to come. I wish to find out who the weaker brethren are!"

*　　　*　　　*

Expectant of the exercise attack, the van of the advance moved into the hills, following the route through a cleft, a narrow valley that wound its way through the folds. The men came out of the heat of the sun for a spell, into a welcome shade. Here, as on the North-West Frontier, no marching force could hope for anonymity, to escape observation from watchers in the peaks, and the column, by order of Brigade, was marching with its music. From the brown hillsides "The Campbells Are Coming" echoed back as the pipes and drums of the Royal Strathspeys beat out. From the fusiliers and from the Bombay Infantry in the rear, picquets, with a sprinkling of Scots, were sent doubling up the hillsides on either hand to watch the heights from the shelter of hastily-built *sangars;* and from the Bombay Infantry a Scots-backed scouting party had been detached earlier, to go ahead at a fast pace and reconnoitre the route for the entry of the main body. The march proceeded; no fall-out for rest had yet been ordered. Black had ridden again down the line for words with Mr Cunningham and the company officers: his strictures had been passed down to the NCOs who had duly instructed their men: this was an exercise but God help anyone who didn't react as though it were the real thing.

The first alarm duly came from the scouting party; a runner was seen coming back at the rush to approach Brigade, and within seconds of his report the bugles were blowing down the column. The voice of the Regimental Sergeant-Major roared at the Scots as the column halted, the commissariat wagons bunching in rear: *"Fall out, clear the pass, take cover where you can!"* In the lead Lord Brora pulled his horse round so sharply that the animal reared on its haunches; and then, accompanied by the Adjutant, he came down the regimental line at a canter, sparks flying as his horses's hooves struck rock in the floor of the pass.

"Look lively, there, you men!" he called. "You're facing a desperate enemy, remember that at all times!" He rode on, passing down the line towards the transport and ammunition column as the Scots scattered off the track to take cover behind rocks and boulders and in crevices. In the lead the Brigade-General had retired with his Brigade Major to a vantage point a little way up the hillside, from where he could watch proceedings and make his assessment. From the direction of the scouts rifle fire was heard, and then a mass of natives, ragged men but uniformed and wearing massive cartridge-filled bandoliers across their chests, was seen to be storming down on the column, a colour party bearing the standard of the Nizam of Hyderal ad. As these men charged along the track, the Royal Bengal Fusiliers covered them with their sights and fired the blanks issued in camp by the *havildars*. From Brigade, the gilded staff watched the bursts, checked the rate of fire and the likelihood of the "enemy" being within killing range. As the Nizam's men stormed along, loosing off live ammunition in a highly dangerous manner, more men appeared over the peaks and dropped down on the picquets in the *sangars*, also firing more or less blindly and yelling like genuine bandits intent upon their marauding affray upon the soldiers of the Raj and the richness of their arsenals. So close did some of the bullets come to the picquets that here and there a man leapt out from cover and physically attacked the "enemy" hand to hand, an unofficial response that drew immediate wrath down upon the Colonels from Brigade. A bugle blew and men froze while the Brigade Major rode down into the track, waving an arm and looking put out.

"I say there, this is an exercise! You men must control yourselves. Will the Commanding Officers kindly take note."

The Brigade Major moved on down the line, still calling his strictures: behind his back, Lord Brora waved his riding-crop threateningly. When the officer had cantered back towards Brigade, the bugle blew again and the exercise was continued in a somewhat half-hearted fashion. At its conclusion the Nizam's men streamed back up the hillsides, melting away fast, and the Colonels were summoned to attend upon the Brigadier-General.

Masefield was in a critical mood. "Disappointing, very," he said. "Your Scots disappointed me most of all, Brora—"

"Why? What was wrong with 'em, may I ask?"

"If you'll give me time to formulate a sentence, Brora, you may certainly ask." Spots of high colour had come to the Brigadier-General's face at Brora's tone. "I noticed a lack of

70

keenness, even dilatoriness. The men seemed to move with a grudge—"

"After, or before, the damn interruption came, sir? To halt an exercise merely to make some damn stupid pettifogging point seems to me to take away any damn sense of reality that may have been there in the first place! Not that there was any reality in any case that I could see. I submit that my men have been used to the real thing, and *charades* make no appeal to them whatsoever."

"I come from the Frontier as well, Lord Brora." Masefield's face was bleak, hard with anger. "Your battalion—"

Brora interrupted again. "On the Frontier, sir, your service was behind a desk. My battalion was engaged in action in the field." Arrogantly Brora pulled his horse round, turning his back upon the Brigadier-General before the latter could retort that he, Lord Brora, had himself but recently arrived in India from his regimental depot in the Scottish Highlands. Masefield's mouth opened and he urged his horse forward, then seemed to change his mind. Brora rode away, back straight, head high, a smirk upon his lips, every lift and fall of his body a studied insult to Brigade. He was almost preening himself as he rejoined his battalion and addressed the Adjutant.

"Damned if I'll have Brigade criticising my men," he said in a loud voice. "We're the best there is, are we not, my dear Black?"

"Indeed, sir, indeed!"

"Then go and tell 'em so."

Black looked surprised. "I beg your pardon, Colonel?"

"I think you heard what I said. You don't propose to argue about it, do you?"

"Oh no, indeed not—"

"Then get on with it. Speak to the Company Commanders and tell them to pass it on." Lord Brora stared along the rock-strewn track, over Black's head. "Here comes a runner from Brigade, demanding my head on a charger, no doubt."

He waited, sitting his horse imperiously as the runner approached and saluted. "Well, what is it, man?"

"From Brigade, sir. The halt will be extended for luncheon, sir."

Brora nodded, and the runner went on his way. Soon the bugles blew again and the cooks unstowed the impedimenta for the field kitchens and set up their stoves and fires. Smells of cooking were wafted on a light breeze. The men, fallen out to rest, lay on the hillsides or sat on boulders, smoking pipes and talking, comparing Southern India with the sterner and more realistic life of the North-West Frontier. As the trestle tables were set up for the officers and laid with freshly starched white cloths, Ogilvie, chatting with a group of fellow company commanders, was joined by Prince George with the Chaplain in tow.

"Well, Padre. Been showing the Prince the ropes, have you?"

"I could scarcely do that, my friend." The Chaplain's long, sallow face remained solemn. "War is not my forte, I fear. Only the results of it when needs be."

"When we're especially glad to have you with us." Ogilvie spoke warmly: the Reverend Hugh MacNab had proved himself a good man, a good friend to the sick, the wounded and the dying. His looks, which were those of a costive and dyspeptic cleric, belied him. He seemed embarrassed by Ogilvie's words, and excused himself from the group of combatant officers, making for a camp stool and mopping at his face with a large white handkerchief. Ogilvie caught the Prince's eye. "You'll have found it tame enough," he said.

"It is hard, on exercises, to make the mind co-operate in the pretence, is it not?"

Ogilvie laughed. "Well said! It is. That's where we're lucky on the Frontier. No pretence up there."

"And no exercises?"

"Not as such, no. We use patrol duty as a training ground for men fresh from home. They learn and fight at the same time, often enough."

72

"I think that is perhaps the better way."

"I'm sure it is," Ogilvie said. A bearer came round, salaaming, taking orders for *chota-pegs*. Ogilvie asked for one for His Royal Highness, one for himself. Taking his from the bearer's tray when it was brought, Prince George clicked his heels together and bowed slightly from the waist.

"Her Majesty the Queen-Empress," he said solemnly, "and His Majesty the Emperor, and the Fatherland."

Taken a little by surprise, Ogilvie nevertheless responded suitably; then glanced at the Prince's almost reverent expression. Drinking, when linked with the loyal toast, was a duty as well as a pleasure: there was preponderant German in Prince George. He might not be a Bismarck's man nor yet a totally devoted soldier; but the militarism was there and would in due course come out. For the Prince's sake, Ogilvie hoped it would, or there would be a sad and possibly disastrous cleavage between his deeply Germanic will to succeed as a soldier and his perhaps equally deep feeling that he would prove weak. As Ogilvie finished the whisky, Black approached, looking formal.

"Captain Ogilvie, you are to tell your Colour-Sergeant to pass to all ranks, we are the best there is. As soldiers, you understand."

Ogilvie stared. "I've a suspicion they know that already, just as all regiments do. What's all this for, all of a sudden?"

"Orders from the Colonel," Black said with a touch of sourness. "All Company Commanders are being similarly instructed." He turned and strode away. Ogilvie, looking sardonic, left the Prince to his whisky and walked down towards where his company was eating dinner. He lifted a hand to Colour-Sergeant MacTrease, who got to his feet, came across smartly, and saluted.

Ogilvie passed the message as ordered. Apparently pleased, MacTrease said, "Aye, sir. Thank you. They'll be pleased to know the Colonel's opinion, sir."

Keeping his fresh surprise out of his face, Ogilvie nodded, returned MacTrease's salute, and walked back towards the luncheon table. Perhaps Lord Brora was after all in closer accord with the men than he was himself. But whether or not this was the case, the Colonel went into something curiously like an about-turn when the alfresco meal was finished, the field kitchens stowed back into the commissariat wagons, and the battalion formed up ready to march out again. Sitting his horse like a rock halfway down the column, he addressed the battalion as a whole.

"Damn poor this morning. Call yourselves fighters? Call yourselves Scots? Good God Almighty, the damn Supply and Transport commanded by a damn *curate* could have done better! You'll pull your socks up sharp from now on or I'll know the reason why, by God! I think you need waking up. Sar'nt-Major?"

Cunningham slammed to attention, marched with kilt a-swing towards the Colonel, halted and saluted. "Sir!"

"We shall wake them up. Until further orders from me, the battalion will advance at the Light Infantry step, at attention, and you shall keep them at it— *smartly!* Do you understand, Sar'nt-Major?"

"Aye, sir."

"Then carry on, if you please." More salutes were exchanged; Cunningham marched away, pace-stick seeming to quiver beneath his arm. His face was angry; it was not the extra physical difficulty of the short Light Infantry step, hell upon earth for tall men, that worried him— after all, the Light Infantry regiments managed it without complaint, though even they would not be expected to maintain it when in marching order in the field; it was the slur that rankled, a slur upon himself as much as upon the NCOs and men. In the same way as in Her Majesty's Navy the ship was the Captain and the Captain the ship, one and indivisible, so was the Regimental Sergeant-Major indivisible from his regiment's smartness and precision. Meanwhile Cunningham passed the word to the colour-sergeants that until further orders the battalion would advance at 140 paces to the minute.

Six

THE SHORT STEP was killing; after an hour three men had
fallen out, two of them from Ogilvie's company. Ogilvie
went ahead to make representations to the Adjutant.

"It is the Colonel's order, Captain Ogilvie, and it has not
yet been rescinded."

"Time it was, then. We're here for exercise, not for the
sick list."

"They'll go on no sick list," Black stated firmly. "You're
aware, are you not, of the Colonel's already stated orders for
those who fall out on the march?"

"Yes, I am," Ogilvie said. He felt sick at heart; to charge a
man with falling out without permission was, under the
circumstances, sheerly heartless; but orders, as ever, had to
be obeyed, and already Colour-Sergeant MacTrease, as
reluctantly as his officer, had taken note of the names. In the
meantime the Brigadier-General was keeping up the
pressure and the rests were few and brief; but within a few
minutes of more men being reported as fallen by the
wayside, Lord Brora passed the order to resume the
regulation pace and the march was thus made easier. Soon
after this came the order to march at ease once again. Ogilvie
hoped there would be singing to lighten the load, but there
was not. There was a good deal of grousing, much of it loud
and intended to be overheard. Ogilvie, hearing well enough,
pretended deafness and advised his subalterns to do
likewise. There was no need to warn MacTrease: that
experienced soldier knew very well when to turn a blind eye.

*　　　*　　　*

They were still in the hills when the daylight left the sky and the Brigadier-General passed the word that he was about to halt the column and send the men into night bivouacs after they had eaten their evening meal. Fallen out, the attention of most of the men was directed towards their feet: washing whenever possible, or at least wiping the toes with a damp cloth, was essential for comfort, since uncleanliness led to excessive sweating. Those who had thus sweated sought permanganate of potash from the medical orderlies for bathing their feet. The socks, when removed, were well stretched and shaken, and when donned again would go on the opposite feet in accordance with the advice contained in the Field Service Pocket Book. Watched over by the picquets on the night-cold hillsides and a strong camp guard in the floor of the pass, a guard provided mainly by the units of Southern Army, the RSM and the RQMS checked the measuring out of the bivouac areas by companies: the shelters were laid in two lines with intervals of two yards between lines and a gangway nine feet wide between left and right half companies, the heads of the sleepers facing front and their rifles at their sides. Ogilvie accompanied the duty subaltern on one of his routine visits to the guard posts that watched protectively over the sleeping battalions. There was, in fact, little for him to criticise; the men of Southern Army were trained soldiers, after all, and there was nothing out of the ordinary in their current duty. All they lacked was action experience. Next morning when the bugles blew Reveille the men roused out sleepily, rubbing eyes, stripping away their night coverings and making their way in shirts and trousers to a stream that ran alongside the track. Here they collected water in mess tins and shaving mugs and, with the aid of mirrors thrust into cleft sticks, carried out their ablutions to the satisfaction of the section sergeants and colour-sergeants. The field kitchens, set up to provide breakfast, also provided hot water for the officers, brought by the bearers to their sahibs. Ogilvie caught a sight of Lord Brora, sitting on the ground in a collarless shirt with the braces of his trews dangling, being obsequiously shaved by his bearer, who looked scared to death that he might draw white blood. Shaving done and his face rinsed and towelled, the Colonel rose to his feet, approached a tin basin of hot water set upon a packing-case, and began a vigorous wash, with soap and water flying about him like a miniature snowstorm. At breakfast some ten minutes later, Lord Brora was in excellent spirits, anticipatory of a good day's march with more exercises interspersed, and giving himself hearty entrenchment in sustaining food. His appetite was quite prodigious: he made short work of fried eggs, liver and bacon, kedgeree, toast and marmalade and many mugs of coffee before lighting a pipe and calling for his thunderbox. He sat and watched as two of his bearers manhandled the field lavatory to a discreet distance off the track and in the lee of some scrubby bushes. He grew talkative.

"Damn fine invention. Must have been damn public in the old days."

"Indeed yes, Colonel." Black, always the sycophant, was the one who made the response.

Brora laughed harshly. "Old Farrar-Drumm would know, of course. I must ask him sometime." He paused. "D'you know, I made a voyage in a sailing-ship once, quite an experience. The master and his mates had more or less decent lavatories, but the crew, by God! They used to down trousers and dangle over the side from ropes and let fly. If a man wasn't seaman enough to eschew the windward side, he had a lesson he was not likely to forget." Brora gave a deep belch and looked round. "By God, Padre, now what's the damn matter? You look green, man! Eat up your breakfast."

"Colonel, I'm afraid I—"

"I said, eat up your breakfast. You need the strength to sit that nag of yours, we have a long day ahead of us and I'm not having the damn Chaplain falling out for lack of his breakfast." Brora got to his feet, slapped at his trews with his cane, and strode off in the wake of the thunderbox.

*   *   *

It was, as promised, a long day and a strenuous one, beginning with the briefings of all ranks. Ogilvie was one of the 114th's officers detailed to attend upon the Bombay Light Infantry while the Viceroy's Commissioned officers were given the *minutiae* of the orders; and he watched while one of these VCOs, sitting by a shelter-tent, passed on the information to his *naiks* and *havildars* who squatted in a half-circle, silent and attentive. Once they were away on the march and clear of the hills, back into the plain again, the men of Southern Army, stiffened by the Highlanders, were sent ahead in groups as extended patrols or ordered to march to the rear until the column was out of sight and then to overtake and mount an attack in the guise of bandits. They were exercised in the duties and skills of vanguard and rearguard and of extended flank cover. At eleven a.m., with the sun blazing down from a hard blue sky, Brigadier-General Masefield's bugler sounded the halt and the main column, minus its detached parties, was fallen out for a rest and a smoke. But as the men sprawled on the ground and pipes were lit, the alarm sounded from the picquets and the battalions were stood to: another attack from the native levies of His Highness the Nizam. The grouses and complaints were many as the Scots lifted themselves from rest and took up their rifles or fed cartridge-belts into the Maxims: it was indeed hard to simulate reality. It had been different on manoeuvres in home commands, in the Monadliath Mountains, on Speyside, or when at Aldershot Camp, Salisbury Plain or the Curragh: then, the majority of the rank and file had never seen real action. Now they were weary of it—ready, indeed, for home again. Not for this caper. When the attack by both infantry and cavalry with artillery support was over, the Scots found it hard to decide who had won. The Nizam's hordes had reached the column and although the spotters and umpires from Brigade stalked about counting "dead" and "wounded", reporting many more such casualties amongst the native force than amongst the defenders, the fact remained that the lumbering elephant-drawn heavy guns had ambled slap into the British line and had those great guns, ancient and unwieldy as they were and very poorly maintained, been loaded with shell or case, then there would surely have been an unholy slaughter of good Scots. On the other hand, had the attack been real, the reaction to it would have been very much sharper, as MacTrease observed to Ogilvie and Prince George.

"In my view, sir, it's a daft carry-on. With respect to the Brigadier-General, sir, of course. The men, sir, have the feeling the staff doesn't know if it's on its arse or its elbow, sir."

"A miscount of casualties, Colour?"

"Something like that, sir, though I have a stronger word for it. Half those told to be dead, sir, were still fighting if that's the way to speak of it. I don't see that it's proving anything, sir, anything at all."

"It's not up to us to question the orders, Colour."

"No, sir. Then if that's all, I'll carry on, sir." MacTrease gave a smart but somewhat offended butt salute on his rifle and marched away. There was a short rest after the exercise had been sorted out by Brigade and then the southward march towards the Kistna River was resumed. At that night's halt for supper and bivouacs, the Colonel had further words to utter to the assembled rank and file in regard to their apparent indifference to the whims of the high command.

"There will be," he announced, "a general tightening up. You all need the fear of God put into you, and into you it will be damn well put!" In the fading light, he stood in his stirrups, his eyes angry, his face commanding and autocratic, like a rock. "I am Lord Brora. I shall not be made a laughing-stock for the miserable native scum of Southern Army. If actual shot be used to stimulate you, to make your lazy feet dance a little, you need not ask whence it came, for it will have come from me." He lifted his riding-crop and struck himself on the chest with its stock, fiercely. "From revolvers in each of these hands of mine, you damn idle dogs! Never say afterwards that you were not warned. I am at the end of my patience. Captain Black!"

"Sir?"

"The men will drill for one hour before their supper. Company officers will be present with their companies."

"*Drill,* Colonel?" Even Black seemed astounded. "In the field?"

"Yes, Captain Black, in the field. Marching and arms drill, to be smartly conducted for one hour even if it grows dark in the meantime." Brora lifted his voice again, once more addressing the whole battalion. "You men. Be ready for the exercise tonight—be ready to repel night attack on the convoy. You're lucky to get the warning in advance, damn me if you're not! A real enemy would not be so obliging." Without more ado Lord Brora pulled his horse round and in the already fading light rode up the Scots column and beyond it, passing the fallen-out sepoys of the Bombay Infantry on his way to Brigade. Behind him the air was blue. Black, shrugging, did his duty, not without a certain pleasure in his face, formally passing the order to the Regimental Sergeant-Major who had already heard it and was unable to prevent himself stating a protest.

"I've never heard the like, sir, never in all my service. The men are tired enough already!"

"They must grow tireder, Mr Cunningham. The order was not mine, you realise that."

"I do, sir, but—"

"There are no 'buts' to an order, Mr Cunningham, as you know well enough, either in the field or elsewhere. You'll take a care not to express your opinions to the NCOs or men."

Cunningham bristled. "That's never been my style, Captain Black, and it'll not become so now—"

"Then kindly keep your voice down, Sar'nt-Major, for already ears are flapping in the ranks."

For once the Regimental Sergeant-Major was nonplussed;

as he struggled for words, the Adjutant turned away, riding his horse slowly to the front. So as not to delay supper for a moment longer than was necessary, the hour's drill was started immediately as the men mustered in companies and the subalterns told off the sections to the drill-sergeants' care. Soon the darkening Indian plain was filled with raucous shouts as the unfortunate Scots marched and wheeled and halted, turned into line and back into file, formed fours, fixed bayonets, presented arms, ordered arms, sloped arms, shouldered arms like Marines aboard ship, who did not slope in case their bayonets should go through the overhead awnings, double-marched with arms at the short trail and swore blasphemously against their Colonel as they did so. As instructed, the Company Commanders remained with their men; so, although it was not necessary, did the Regimental Sergeant-Major, pausing in an angry promenade to speak to Ogilvie.

"I am not a disloyal man, Captain Ogilvie, sir, but . . ." He paused, his face working.

Ogilvie laid a hand on his broad shoulder. "Spill it, Bosom. Relieve the pressure or you'll explode. It'll go no further."

"Yes, sir. Thank you." Cunningham tugged at his Sam Browne belt, spread like a seaboat's griping-band across the immensity of his chest. "I have a strong wish to see Lord Dornoch back with us. His Lordship is a fine Colonel, the very best."

Ogilvie grinned. "All right, I take your point. You're the soul of discretion, Bosom! But it's no use wishing the impossible, is it?"

"No, indeed it is not." Cunningham sighed. "All the same . . . and it's not just because of the peccadilloes . . . I'm worried about the regiment."

"Why's that?"

"They'll not fight the same way, sir. Not for Lord Brora as for Lord Dornoch is what I mean. It's a different style of leadership now, sir, more like driving, and that never works with Scots. They don't need it and they don't like it."

"I know. But fighting's not on the menu, is it?"

"Not for a while, no. But there's been talk—official talk from the Colonel—that it could come. I'll tell you what I think, sir, how I assess the situation—if you wish to hear, that is?"

"Please go on, Bosom. Your opinion's always of value —and you know I mean that."

"Aye, sir, I do." There was affection as well as respect in Cunningham's voice. He had served in the regiment with Sir Iain Ogilvie in his time, had watched, indeed nursed, the young James from his subaltern days, had seen his officer grow from his Sandhurst freshness to an experienced and reliable and considerate Frontiersman, a good Company Commander who invariably saw to his men's needs before his own comfort. Between RSM and Captain there was a bond of friendship forged in the heat of action as well as in the day-to-day routines of cantonment life. Cunningham went on, "All told, sir, there are three brigades marching on the Kistna River. Nine battalions, with guns, support troops, stores, equipment, ammunition, wagons and transport animals. And a whole Division waiting up in Secunderabad for possible use as reinforcements, as I take it. It's quite a lot of men, sir."

"It's to be a large-scale exercise, Bosom. Or are you suggesting a deeper motive?"

"Aye, I am that, Captain Ogilvie. It's down by the Kistna this rebel Rajah's said to be massing support." Cunningham paused. "It would seem clear enough to any thinking man that there's a connection—and that it'll not be *exercises* we'll be on, except maybe as a feint."

"The point hasn't escaped my notice, Bosom, I assure you. But the Colonel will keep us informed, you know. He's not proved slow to do that so far."

"Aye, sir, I agree as to that."

Ogilvie sounded puzzled. "What's your worry? We don't mind a spot of real action, do we?"

"Indeed we do not, sir. Though it's likely to prove more than just a spot. Nor will we mind all that much pulling the Nizam's chestnuts out of the fire for him. But I go back to my earlier point, sir: the men are in no mood to pull any chestnuts for Lord Brora."

"I see," Ogilvie said in a thoughtful tone. "That's your considered opinion, Bosom?"

Cunningham said stoutly, "It is, sir."

"But they'll do their duty, obey their orders?"

"Indeed they will, sir. I'm not suggesting mutiny! But they'll be sullen about it, and sullen men don't extend themselves unduly."

"I'm not sure you're right," Ogilvie said. "Once they're in action, they won't hold back. That's human nature."

"Well, sir, I'd not bank too far on it. There's a curious feeling . . . it's not all the Colonel. It's as though, now we've left the Frontier for a spell, the spring's unwound. Do you follow me, sir?"

Ogilvie nodded. "I think so. They've thought themselves into an easy billet! A holiday in a sense. If that's the case, hasn't it occurred to you that the Colonel may also have sensed it, and is acting to keep them in full fighting trim?"

"Aye, sir, that thought has occurred I'll admit. But there are ways, and ways."

"Perhaps. But I have another feeling, and it's this: action of itself will rewind the spring, Bosom! If it doesn't . . ." He shrugged.

"If it doesn't," Cunningham said ominously, "it'll be too late. I was wondering, Captain Ogilvie, if a tactful word could not be dropped into the Colonel's ear before that happens? A word that—"

Ogilvie broke in with a laugh. "My good Bosom, have you ever tried dropping a tactful word into the ear of a mule?" He pulled himself up sharply, cursing himself for an indiscretion. "Forget that, Sar'nt-Major."

"I failed to hear it, sir, quite failed indeed. But I'll leave it up to you, sir." The Regimental Sergeant-Major gave a cough and pulled his shoulders square, lifting his head to look at the sky. "No light left to speak of, sir. But five minutes of drill to go," he added as he pulled out his watch. "They'd never believe this . . ." His voice died away into another cough; Ogilvie grinned to himself, guessing that Cunningham had been about to utter an indiscretion of his own—that they would never believe it at the depot in Invermore; but of course they would, for Lord Brora had but recently come from there himself . . .

*   *   *

Lord Brora had the more recently come from Brigade as it happened: it was a brief visit to Masefield's bivouac and he had returned by the time the officers' evening meal was announced. Ogilvie was sent for; and found the Colonel seated on a camp stool with Black in attendance.

Brora, who was drinking whisky in the light of a storm lantern hanging from a pole stuck in the ground, lost no time in coming to the point. "Ogilvie, I'm instructed by the Brigadier-General to exercise a mixed patrol of the native units with Scots backing. A probe towards where we estimate our notional enemy to be positioned ready for their attack. Do you understand?"

"Yes, Colonel. What, precisely, will the orders be?"

Brora waved a hand; the glowing end of a cigar cut a swathe in the darkness. "To approach and observe the Nizam's niggers— without being observed yourselves. Then to return and report their distance, bearing and numbers. You'll be in charge, and you may select six of your privates with a sergeant and corporal. All personnel will be armed with live ammunition, just in case of bandits, real ones." He snapped his fingers. "The map, if you please, Black."

Black unrolled a map and held it below the storm lantern. Lord Brora leaned across and beckoned to Ogilvie. "There," he said, stubbing a finger onto the map. "That's where

84

Brigade expects to find 'em. And we're *here.*" Down came the finger again. "Lay off a course on your compasses and close the buggers. Easy enough in basis, but remember the purpose: to exercise the Bombay and Bengal sepoys— thus it'll be an unwieldy patrol for you to command. You're to take thirty from each regiment, thirty sepoys that is, with appropriate *naiks* and *havildars.* A native officer will be detailed from each regiment. Understood, Ogilvie?"

Ogilvie acknowledged his understanding of the orders but appeared to be hesitating; Brora said impatiently, "Well, get on with it, then! I want you away as soon as dinner's over. Report to the Adjutant when you're ready."

"Yes, Colonel. There's one thing, if I may ask it—"

"Oh, come on, man!"

"His Royal Highness, Colonel. May I take him as my second-in-command? He'd appreciate the experience, I know."

Brora glared. "What damn use would he be, for God's sake? He's not of our army. I'm not in the least interested in giving him experience. You'll take your senior subaltern as your second-in-command, d'you hear?"

"Yes, Colonel. But perhaps as a supernumerary—"

"Oh, the devil take you!" Brora seemed to lose interest. He waved an arm in the air. "Take him, take him! So long as he's not accorded any standing, or military command, he can balance upside down in a bucket of water for all I care. Take him and go. He's not to have that damn manservant what's-his-name with him, though, I'll not have that bugger in any patrol of mine. Feller's as pale as butter and looks like a damn spy— a typical square-head Hun. And remember this: the Prince is your personal responsibility, no one else's."

"That's understood, Colonel. Thank you." Ogilvie saluted and turned about. As he marched away he already half regretted his sudden impulse: Prince George was with the regiment as a guest and would appreciate the opportunity of seeing something that might be more interesting than the mere accompaniment of a column on the march; but he would certainly be a hindrance, a hindrance that would need everything explained as they went along. However, the matter had now been decided. Reaching his company's lines where the men were waiting for their mess tins to be filled with supper, Ogilvie found MacTrease and passed the orders.

"I'll take Sar'nt Davison and Corporal Dougal. I'll leave the choice of men to you, Colour. In the meantime I'll contact the Adjutants of the native regiments and ask them to send their parties to report to you."

"Very good, sir." MacTrease saluted. Ogilvie went off about his business before going for his own meal. When he attended for supper he found Prince George chatting with a bunch of officers. The Prince seemed pleased at his suggestion, though with some reservation that he might be in the way; Ogilvie assured him that he would not and that his company would be very welcome. During supper he gave the Prince an outline of the conduct of a night probe against enemy lines, stressing the need for absolute silence in the last stages of the approach and the need to keep eyes skinned for outpost sentries and picquets. As soon as they had finished the meal Ogilvie and Prince George walked down to where MacTrease was mustering the men of the patrol: there were two Viceroy's Commissioned Officers present, a *jemadar* as ordered from each native battalion.

Ogilvie introduced himself and said, smiling as he shook their hands, "I'm delighted you're coming with me, though I think you'll put me in an invidious position!"

"Why is that, sahib?" one of them asked.

Ogilvie laughed and bent to adjust his equipment. "This is your country, and you must know it a great deal better than I! Perhaps we shall each learn from the other." He turned to his sergeant. "Sar'nt Davison?"

"Sir!"

"Stand the men at ease, if you please." The order was passed. Ogilvie indicated the purpose and scope of the patrol, emphasising the necessity for the Scots in particular to remember that the live ammunition in the magazines of their rifles was on no account to be used other than on his personal order. "Keep it in mind that the Frontier's a long way north," he said. "There could be bandits, but in fact it's much more likely that any flitting shadows in the night will be men of the Nizam's army, probably doing the same as us. We don't want any accidents. I hope that's clear." He paused, looking down the line of men as they waited beneath the light of a storm lantern the beams of which reflected from brass buttons and equipment and, dully, from the barrels of the Lee-Enfield rifles and the scabbarded side-arms. He moved away to report to Black. Returning, he said crisply, "I have orders to be back with the column by midnight. The Nizam's force is said to be five miles distant, so we should reach their outpost sentries in a little over an hour." He glanced at his sergeant. "Carry on, Sar'nt Davison."

"Sir!" The orders were given and the patrol marched out in twos, their rifles slung from their left shoulders, the British and Indian NCOs giving the step until they were clear of the bivouacs. Ogilvie marched in the lead with Prince George of Hohenzollern alongside him; halfway down the column marched the two *jemadars,* and in rear was Ogilvie's senior subaltern, Lieutenant Bruce Fraser, with Davison and a *havildar* from the Bombay Infantry having a roving mission up and down the line. Following his compass bearing, reading the dial in the light of matches struck in the shelter of cupped hands, Ogilvie led the patrol silently across the Indian plain, making fast progress. When about half the distance had been covered towards the Nizam's force, the clouds, driven by a stiff breeze, parted to reveal the moon sailing in majesty across the brooding sky that was heavy with clustered stars. Ogilvie cursed the moonlight as it spread its silver over the ground, bringing up the occasional stunted tree or scrubby bush or mound of earth. If that moon continued on its stately way, a patrol the size of this one, so inordinately large for its task of spotting the "enemy", would be picked up by the

Nizam's perimeter guards long before it could make any observations.

As quietly as possible Ogilvie passed the word back to halt. As the column came to a stop in some bush cover Sergeant Davison reported for orders, doubling up from the rear.

"My compliments to Mr Fraser, Sar'nt Davison. The patrol's to split laterally into groups of four, each group to maintain fifty yards between itself and the next on either side, and all to follow me." He pointed. "Ahead there, there's a ridge with a defile running centrally through it—see it?"

"I see it, sir."

"We'll advance on the ridge. At a guess it's about a mile ahead. We re-form in its cover and enter the defile and I'll reconnoitre from there, all right?"

"Aye, sir."

"We should find the native positions not too far beyond, I fancy. From there, we'll need to advance on our stomachs."

"Very good, sir. But I'd suggest, sir, that we do that now. The Nizam's force will likely have a picquet out on the ridge."

Ogilvie looked up at the sky. "It'll not be necessary. There's cloud forming and we'll be in darkness presently. We'll wait till we are and we'll move out without further orders the moment the moon goes—that'll be the signal." He paused. "I take your point about a picquet, though. Instead of re-forming, we'll outflank the ridge, Sar'nt."

"Splitting in two halves, sir, one right and the other left flank?"

"Right! Re-form on the far side, and cut off the whole ridge. I'll take all six of the 114th's privates directly through the defile myself and hope to take prisoners." Ogilvie turned to the *jemadars,* who had now joined the conference. "I'd like one of you to take command of the left advance, the other of the right. I'll send my sergeant with one group, my corporal with the other. Fraser sahib will keep a general eye

88

on all sections till the ridge is abreast and between the two main flank advances. Clear, gentlemen?"

Their nods gave the affirmative; Ogilvie told Sergeant Davison to rejoin Fraser and detail the groups of four, reporting when he had done so. He added a warning, chiefly for the benefit of the native officers: "Remember this is an exercise, and remember what I said earlier about your live rounds." Five minutes later the six privates of the Royal Strathspey reported in, followed by Davison reporting all groups told off. Ogilvie put a hand on Prince George's arm. "Keep with me and my Scots. It should be a bit of fun for you if we flush the picquets." Just then the moon sailed behind heavy cloud to leave a blank darkness in which little could be seen; from now on, at least until the moon reappeared, they would have to trust to their sense of direction. Acting upon his order to Davison that the moon's extinction should be the signal, Ogilvie came out from his cover with his party and doubled ahead, stumbling through the darkness towards the distant ridge with the German prince at his side. To right and left the Indian Army units with their small stiffening of Scots NCOs also moved on at the double, all of them trying to beat the moon, Ogilvie's subaltern doubling up behind them. The darkness began to lose some of its intensity as the moon neared the ragged edges of the cloud bank, and a few moments later it sailed out into view once more, roundly bright, to make every landmark stand clearly out. All the men dropped flat and the advance went on as a stomach-crawl, slow and painful. But there was more cloud around and the breeze was blowing yet; once again the light went as the moon disappeared. The dispersed soldiers got to their feet and ran ahead, beginning to diverge further to left and right, with Ogilvie keeping to his central position. Before the ridge was reached, there was one more period of moonlight, enough to show the patrol that they were on target. Now that they were close there was a feeling of hidden menace about the ridge: it lay like some sleeping, humped animal across their path, an unmoving

89

guard-dog between them and their quarry, but a dog that could turn very noisy and dangerous once disturbed. And it carried its fleas: glints of moonlight were clear indication of *jezails* and their long, snaky bayonets, while here and there, as if in confirmation, a turbaned head showed briefly. From his position on the ground, flattened and covered by coarse grass and scrub, Ogilvie lifted his head a little: the outflanking forces could not be seen, but by now he assessed that they would be close to their objectives at each end of the ridge. As for himself and his small force, they would have little more than a couple of hundred yards to cover in a final dash for the entry to the defile the moment the light went again. When it did so Ogilvie lost no time: in a whisper he gave his last order to his handful of Scots. "Through the defile, mop up what we find, and join the Indian units at the other end. We'll march the Nizam's men on with us, after they've been bound and gagged. Once we've reconnoitred, we return to bivouacs." He paused. "Right. Here we go!"

They got up and ran for the defile, moving swifly and in silence. If he could capture some of the Nizam's force, they could be questioned at Brigade, Ogilvie assumed, always provided interrogation was carried out in accordance with the rules, whatever they might be, for exercise. No physical pressure could be applied; but deft questioning by the Political Officer attached to Brigade could produce results. That should please Lord Brora, if anything could ever please him . . . Reaching the defile, apparently undetected, the small force came into a darkness that seemed and felt deeper than ever: the enclosing sides shut them in, surrounding them like the walls of the grave itself. Immediately alongside him, Ogilvie heard the intake of breath from Prince George: German he might be, the Uhlan Guard his regiment—but even on an exercise he seemed to be feeling the innate lonely eeriness of the sub-continent, the inescapable atmosphere of latent evil that made a man cast glances constantly over his shoulder . . . as the Prince sent a stone flying Ogilvie reached out and squeezed his arm. "The going's rough underfoot," he whispered into his ear, "but silence is the order of the day—or night. Try not to stumble."

"I am sorry, James."

"It's all right, I don't think they—" His words were seized from his mouth and tossed as it were into the jaws of hell. From right ahead and seemingly above them came a blast of flame, red and white and orange, a tremendous crash accompanied by searing heat, and a whistle, a scream that died away overhead. Then from the high sides of the defile, so like a miniature version of the Khyber Pass into Afghanistan, came the flash and crack of rifles, and as pieces of rock began to fly about his ears Ogilvie realised that the Nizam's men were not firing blanks.

Seven

FROM IMMEDIATELY BEHIND him Ogilvie heard the voice of one of his Scots, Private Innes. "Do we open, sir?"

"No. They're taking us for bandits, but I'm not staying to argue the toss." Ogilvie raised his voice in a shout to the others. "Hold your fire—continue through the defile at the double. Fast as you can go!" He doubled ahead himself, plunging into almost total darkness pinpricked by the flashes above as the natives on the high sides of the defile maintained their fire. Their aim was wild and they had no more light than he; Ogilvie had little doubt that his small force would get though intact to join up with the main bodies of the patrol as they outflanked the ridge. He was gripped by rising fury: panic action on the part of the Nizam's men was something neither he nor Lord Brora had taken into account, but Lord Brora could be relied upon to cause the rolling of a few native heads after this! Ogilvie pounded on, slithering, stumbling, just managing to keep his feet with his Scots coming on close in his rear. The firing continued but seemed now to be dropping behind, as though the native troops were still firing straight down into the mouth of the defile where last the Scots had been caught; and it was only a matter of minutes before Ogilvie's group came clear of the enclosing sides and found themselves out into the plain and apparently intact. Once again there was a little moonlight, and in it Ogilvie saw the two outflanking forces moving in to join up with him. Distantly ahead, he saw more figures: riders coming down from the Nizam's encampment, no doubt to enquire into the cause of the firing.

Bruce Fraser came up with Sergeant Davison and asked what had happened.

"Took us for bandits, obviously," Ogilvie answered. "I was tempted to return their fire, but—" He turned as the Nizam's cavalry approached. The leading horseman pulled his horse up and stared down, his face hawklike beneath the turban. Ogilvie spoke coldly: "Do your men always open fire with live ammunition during an exercise?"

The native raised heavy eyebrows. "You are from the British force with whom we exercise?"

"Yes, and—"

"I am from the Nizam's army as you have suggested. Was it you who fired?"

"Certainly not!" Ogilvie snapped. "I'm asking—"

"Then you were fired upon. Do you know by whom?"

"By your men, clearly!"

The man shook his head. "Not so. We have no outpost so far extended." He paused, letting his words sink in. "You, sahib, have led your men into a trap set by bandits—or by rebels, followers of the renegade, the Rajah of Rangapore!"

Ogilvie stared, his mouth open, feeling his face flush to the roots of his hair. He had been criminally negligent in his assessment, in his first reaction: the obvious had not once occurred to him. His mind had been too set in a single track, the track that had told him the ridge must be held by the Nizam's sepoys. Brora himself had made mention of possible bandits, real ones, whose hypothetical presence had been the reason for the issue of live ammunition. Ogilvie could feel accusation in the air: but at least no casualties had been inflicted. He was consoling himself with this thought when the bombshell came. Sergeant Davison approached, halted, and saluted.

"Captain Ogilvie, sir. His Royal Highness, sir. The German prince . . . he's no longer with us."

*   *   *

The moonlight streamed down across the plain now, all cloud having scudded away on a rising wind. Everything stood out clearly, including the detachment of the Royal Strathspeys moving out towards the ridge with artillery support. Ahead of them rode the gaunt figure of Andrew Black, who spurred his horse as soon as he saw the oncoming patrol, and reined in beside Ogilvie.

"Well, Captain Ogilvie, is our assistance wanted? What happened? The gunfire was heard."

"Was it?" Ogilvie's voice was dull and expressionless.

Black stared. "What's the matter, my dear fellow?"

"I've lost Prince George."

"*What?*"

Ogilvie reported what had happened, each word an effort of will. "When I was joined by the Nizam's cavalry, we attacked the ridge in strength. Result, nil. The bandits, or the Rajah's men if that's who they were—they'd gone."

"Gone? Not a trace, d'you mean, nothing to pursue?"

"Nothing at all. Of course, I carried out a general reconnaissance. I found nothing—"

"No tracks?"

"On this ground? No, no tracks."

"And then?"

Ogilvie said, "I decided to return and report. The Nizam's levies are continuing the search, but no one's hopeful of results."

"I see. And the Prince?"

"Dead," Ogilvie answered, indicating a burden being carried by four Scots. "We found his body in the defile. I'm taking him back to the column."

"I see," Black said again, his voice solemn and seeming filled with foreboding. "The exercise, Captain Ogilvie, the night attack by the Nizam's men—what of that now?"

"I've dealt with that. I took it upon myself to tell the levies to ride back with word that it was cancelled."

"Yes." Black nodded. "In the circumstances—a royal tragedy—I would say you did quite right in that respect." He

94

looked out over the plain towards the ridge, standing stark and lonely beneath the moon. "Very well, Captain Ogilvie, we shall return to bivouacs—and face the Colonel."

*   *   *

The march back was a miserable affair of defeat and personal recrimination for Ogilvie, a march conducted in silence except for the rattle of arms and equipment and the creak of leather. In the centre of the original patrol, the four men of the 114th Highlanders carried the body of the dead Prince between them, with Sergeant Davison marching reverently in rear. That march seemed never-ending. As they entered the battalion's lines Lord Brora was seen standing outside his bivouac, his large frame lit by a guard lantern that guttered in the cold wind, guttered with yellow flickers that cast weird shadows over the rocky ground and the hillside behind him. Black stood the men easy, dismounted, and walked over towards the Colonel. After a lengthy conversation during which Lord Brora drew himself straighter and stiffer, as it seemed, at each word, Black called out to Ogilvie to report. Ogilvie marched forward, halted in front of the Colonel, and saluted.

Brora's eyes seemed to search his soul. "Well, Captain Ogilvie, you seem to have distinguished yourself. It is not every officer who can claim to have lost a prince! Kindly explain yourself."

"I shall, Colonel." Ogilvie made a detailed report, an honest report with nothing omitted and with no attempt to excuse himself beyond the assertion that he had thought the men on the ridge to be the Nizam's advanced outpost.

"Thought!" Brora sneered openly. "I require my officers not to think, but to know. That is what the men expect also. Leadership presupposes knowledge, my dear sir, not damn thought! You're lucky not to have more casualties to report."

95

"I realise that, Colonel."

"And His Royal Highness?"

"I'm very sorry, Colonel."

"And are about to become a damn sight sorrier. He was your responsibility. Do you not remember that I made that point very particularly, Captain Ogilvie, before you left?"

"Yes, Colonel."

Brora caught Black's eye. "You heard that?"

"It has been noted, Colonel."

"Good. Now, Captain Ogilvie, for the third time you have been slow to open fire when the need arose, for the third time, no less, you have in effect disregarded my expressed orders. This is something to be deplored in any officer, and especially in any officer of my regiment, which is a proud and glorious one. Its name is never to be sullied by any disinclination to engage—"

"Colonel, I—"

"Be silent, sir, hold your damn tongue!" Brora's face seemed to swell with angry blood, and his body moved as though he was restraining himself with difficulty from striking Ogilvie. "Reluctance, cowardice, belting off to safety and leaving an honoured guest to be killed . . . bah! I have no further words—"

"Sir, I must—"

"And if you're wise, neither have you, sir! I shall report the facts to the Brigadier-General at once. In the meantime, you will consider yourself in arrest and confined to your bivouac until sent for. Captain Black, kindly make the necessary arrangements. A captain as escort. Then I'll see Mr Fraser, Sar'nt Davison, Corporal Dougal and those two *jemadars,* as well as the men who entered that defile with Ogilvie." Pointedly, Lord Brora turned his back; with murder in his heart, Ogilvie gave it a frigid salute. When he turned, he found Black by his side.

"Your pardon, James, but I am now required to accompany you until someone else has been detailed. I would appreciate it if you would make my duty easy for me."

"I'm not going to knock you down and run for it, if that's what you're fearing," Ogilvie said as they moved away.

Black smiled oilily. "Oh, come, James! You know very well—"

"Is Brora thinking of a Court Martial?"

"Really, I can't say what's in the Colonel's mind, can I? Get some sleep, that's my advice. There's no point in brooding, you know, James. What's to be, will be—and you have a good record to date." Black shook his head sadly as they walked on towards Ogilvie's bivouac .past officers bedding down once again after the recent alarm. "Mind, if there's to be a Court Martial, it's not likely to be a *field* one, and I dare say you know what I mean by saying that—do you not?"

"Yes," Ogilvie answered abruptly. As an officer he could be tried only by a General Court Martial or a Field General Court Martial, the latter being convened only for such offences as it was not practicable to try by the ordinary process; and if he was to go before a General Court Martial it would almost certainly be in Ootacamund—in the close proximity of General Farrar-Drumm who had himself committed Prince George to his personal care. It was not a happy thought; and Ogilvie was in fact only too ready to blame himself for the appalling lack of mental alertness that had led to the young German's death. Prince George had wanted so desperately to prove himself and to live to enjoy the freedom, whilst in India, that he had not been permitted in the German court. All that was over now. Within half an hour of leaving Lord Brora, Ogilvie was sent for to attend upon Brigade with his escorting officer—Robin Stuart, who in the meantime had relieved Black. Once again, in his Colonel's presence, he told his story. Masefield's face was grave and formidable throughout, much troubled in the lantern's light. When Ogilvie had finished he said, "The blame for this is not for me to lay. Your Colonel, your acting Colonel I should say, has asked for a Court Martial and I'm bound to say I agree with him. I shall forward my approval together with his request. The matter will be decided at Southern Command, of course, but I have no doubt of that decision. Have you anything further you wish to say, Captain Ogilvie, at this stage?"

"No, thank you, sir. Except to say I'm deeply sorry."

"Quite, quite. I truly believe you, my dear fellow." Masefield coughed. "It's most unfortunate—most unfortunate. You'll appreciate the position, I know. A Prince of the German Empire—the repercussions could be immense, even world shattering—a royal guest of the British Army, killed in a foray whilst under military protection! But I'll say no more. You may go, Captain Ogilvie."

"Sir!" Ogilvie gave a smart salute and turned about with a stamp of boots. Accompanied by Stuart, he marched away, down the lines to his own battalion and his bivouac, feeling wakeful eyes upon him as he passed in the disgrace of arrest. As he reached the Scots line an embarrassing incident took place: Klaus Knicken, the dead Prince's manservant, came forward suddenly from behind a rock, his eyes blazing with hate. Running up to Ogilvie before Stuart could stop him, he burst out into a torrent of German and spat full in Ogilvie's face. He was dragged away by three privates and a lance-corporal, shouting still.

"Easy with him," Ogilvie called, his face white and stiff. "It wasn't his fault." He marched on with Stuart, passed Andrew Black who avoided his eye. Making for his bivouac he turned in but found no sleep. Dawn came at last, came on wings that dragged in the Indian dust. The bugles blew Reveille and the soldiers came out of their shelters, shivering, stamping feet, flailing arms about their bodies to drive away the night's chills. The smell of breakfast cooking arose, stealing temptingly over the lines of men as they washed and shaved with a frugal care for the available water, for here there was no handy stream to use for the ablutions. Ogilvie, sitting up and looking pale and drawn, glanced down at Robin Stuart emerging from a bivouac at his side. Meeting his eye, Stuart read Ogilvie's expression.

"Try to keep it out of your mind, old boy," he said kindly.

"How can I? Everyone will know by now, the whole Brigade'll be buzzing like flies on a dung-heap!"

"Perhaps." Stuart sighed. "But don't forget our chaps all know bloody Brora too!" He got to his feet and dusted down his uniform. "When we go to breakfast, just keep more or less in my vicinity, won't you, James? I ask no more than that."

"I know. Thank you, Robin. You've always been a good friend."

Stuart looked embarrassed. "No need to use the past tense, old boy." Ogilvie made no reply, deep again in his own bitter reflections on how easily this whole wretched business could have been avoided: if only—to start with—he'd never suggested the Prince might accompany the patrol! It had been his own idea entirely; no doubt at the Court Martial Brora would make much of that. After breakfast, taken early with the day's march towards the Kistna in mind, men passed and re-passed as the battalion made ready. After some comings and goings between Brora and the brigade staff, Ogilvie was visited by Andrew Black with his orders: in view of the exceptional circumstances, of the dead man's rank and importance, Brigadier-General Masefield was taking the unusual course of sending Ogilvie back forthwith to Secunderabad, under escort, to await the pleasure of Sir Clarence Farrar-Drumm who would for a certainty order a Court Martial to be convened post-haste so that the fullest reports could be made swiftly to His Excellency the Viceroy in Calcutta and to Her Majesty's Government in Whitehall, to say nothing of the court of the German Emperor himself. Her Majesty, said Black ominously, would take personal note of an albeit distant loss suffered by her Imperial grandson. With Ogilvie would go Lord Brora himself, as prosecuting officer, together with Lieutenant Fraser, Ogilvie's second-in-command at the relevant time, Sergeant Davison, Corporal Dougal, the six privates of the defile party, and the *jemadars* from the native

99

regiments. The battalion, though in a sense in the field, was not engaged in action but only in manoeuvres; Lord Brora could in the special circumstances be spared from his command, which now devolved upon Black. It was true enough, Black agreed, that action could come, and indeed last night had proved beyond doubt that the rebel Rajah of Rangapore was on the move, but if the need arose Lord Brora could be ridden back from Secunderabad or entrained from Coimbatore to an en route station. In the meantime a rider had come in from the Nizam's army with a report that the continued search had revealed nothing and that the area appeared clear of rebel forces.

"What about the body?" Ogilvie asked in a low voice.

"Not needed as evidence, since the facts are well known and vouched for. You know India, James. The burial's to take place at once, before the regiment moves out. There's nothing else for it. The heat's the last enemy." Black took out a handerkerchief and blew his nose, as though already wafting away the smell of corruption from his nostrils. "The man Knicken will ride with you and your party, to report to Ootacamund for onward transit to Germany."

*   *   *

In the van the pipes and drums played the regiment out of bivouacs and onward for the Kistna River. Behind the pipers and drummers and behind the Brigadier-General rode Captain Andrew Black, acting grandly in command. A salute was given as the head of the long column passed the lonely cairn-topped grave of Prince George of Hohenzollern, with the flag of Germany, hastily run up by the regimental tailor from scraps of cloth, floating on the wind from a pole thrust into the ground at the head. Earlier, Ogilvie had heard the discharge of the firing party and the sad wail of a Highland lament on the pipes, had heard them with a pricking behind his eyelids. Up the Scots column strode the Regimental Sergeant-Major and the colour-sergeants, calling the step and using pace-sticks until the order should come down from Brigade to march at ease. Drawn to one side was Lord Brora with the mounted party for Secunderabad. Ogilvie watched the battalion march out. As the sound of the pipes faded, his heart was like lead: if action should come, the only place for him was with the Royal Strathspey. The passing Scots gave an eyes-left in salute to Lord Brora, and as his hand came down from the acknowledgment the Colonel gave the order for his mounted column to form for the ride to Secunderabad, which should take little more than a day. His face was like granite as he stared at Ogilvie.

"A fine night's work indeed, Captain Ogilvie! You've been responsible for denuding your regiment of its Colonel and of officers and men needed in action. I trust you're proud of that."

"I was guilty of no more than a faulty appreciation of the position, Colonel."

"Hold your damn tongue, sir! I demand a clean regiment. It's the only way to fight." The Colonel lifted his right hand in the executive order to move out, and brought it down again viciously. The ride of disgrace began, with Lord Brora in the lead. He rode with a swagger, with an almost insane pride. Ogilvie felt physically sick.

Eight

UPON ARRIVAL IN Secunderabad the party was attached for
accommodation to a native regiment of fusiliers in cantonments; Ogilvie was allotted a quarter to be shared with
Robin Stuart, who was still to be his constant companion.
His worries grew upon themselves: as yet, he had been given
no idea as to how the charge might be framed. Dereliction of
duty, disobedience of orders, failure to engage the enemy,
even cowardice? Although made a temporary member of the
Officers' Mess, Ogilvie kept to his quarter and asked for
meals to be sent in. Stuart, in disregard of regulations,
arranged with the native NCO in charge of the Mess servants
to send in whisky, and Ogilvie inc' ·ged in more *chota pegs*
than usual: when morning came, he had a sore head and a
dry mouth. Morning also brought orders, conveyed to him
via Lord Brora through Robin Stuart: a despatch had been
sent on the telegraph to Southern Army in Ootacamund, a
coded message giving full details, and General Farrar-
Drumm had lost no time in making his reply. This reply read:

> Court Martial will be convened under my presidency
> soonest possible after your arrival Ootacamund. Prison-
> er, escort, prosecuting officer and witnesses are to
> entrain immediately for Ootacamund. Governor
> Madras Presidency and HE have been informed, like-
> wise Commander-in-Chief and GOC Northern Army.

"So my father knows," Ogilvie said bitterly.

"That was inevitable, wasn't it?" Stuart's face was
concerned, compassionate. "Look, old man. He had to
know. We're still part of Northern Army, after all."

"Yes, true." Ogilvie got up from where he was sitting and walked across to the shuttered window. He pushed the shutters back and stared across the verandah towards the parade-ground, where the *naiks* and *havildars* were drilling their sections. A familiar enough scene—too familiar; if things went wrong in Ootacamund it could be one he would not see again. There was a ring about the whole of the proceedings to date that spoke in a loud voice of a verdict of Guilty; and in his heart Ogilvie knew that in fact that would be a true verdict; to fail to make a proper appreciation of a situation was a military sin. Had there been no casualties, of course, it would scarcely have led to a Court Martial; his Colonel could have dealt with the matter with a few acid words and a notation on his record. But with a royal personage dead, and a German at that, a trial was inevitable and no court would be likely to acquit. Ogilvie gave a sigh of near despair. Turning, he said, "I wonder if it's all worthwhile, Robin."

"What?"

"The regiment, the army itself. It'll never be the same again, whatever happens."

"It's your life, James. You'd be miserable if you gave it up."

Ogilvie laughed harshly. "It looks like giving me up, doesn't it?"

"Never say die, old man."

"Platitudes!"

"Look here, James. It's not all over, you know. It won't help you to think that way." Stuart, sitting in a basket-chair by the screened doorway, stared up at him. "Everything depends on the wording of the charge, doesn't it? You'll simply have to wait for that."

"There'll be the alternative charges. Always something to get one on, if the first charge fails."

"Oh, for God's sake," Stuart said wearily. "The British Army has its faults, but it's not that vindictive. They're not going to be out to get you if they don't find you at fault—"

103

"Senior officers don't like taking the blame if they can shift it, Robin."

"Some, I agree—not all. Not your father, for example. And I think you ought to remember one thing: in this case no one else happened to be remotely responsible."

"D'you mean—"

"I mean what I said and no more, James my boy!" Stuart got to his feet and faced Ogilvie, laying his hands on the other's shoulders and looking him in the eye. "It's hell to live with, I realise, but you must face it: if you'd reacted faster and returned that fire . . . Prince George just might not have died. It's not a case where anyone's going to try to shift the responsibility—for God's sake, keep that in mind! You'll get a fair trial and you've got to stop feeling quite so bloody sorry for yourself."

*   *   *

They were entrained for the south within the hour, en route for Coimbatore. At Coimbatore they transferred to the mountain railway and in Ootacamund were met by military transport that took them straight to Southern Army Headquarters. Lord Brora was taken by an aide-de-camp into General Farrar-Drumm's presence while the rest of the party remained in a corridor, Ogilvie and his escort being told to wait in an ante-room. Ogilvie sat beneath portraits of great men, statesmen and soldiers who through the long years of the Raj had governed India and kept the Pax Britannica in being. They seemed to gaze down upon him with stern disapproval and upbraiding, the officer who had let the side down and involved the Queen-Empress in personal distress: Clive of India, Warren Hastings, Lord William Bentinck, Cornwallis, Wellesley, Minto, Dalhousie, Canning . . . Mayo, Lytton, Ripon. A formidable bunch, with old-fashioned faces, men of principle and a high sense of duty and responsibility.

104

The ADC returned. "The General will see you now, Ogilvie." He glanced at Robin Stuart. "Alone."

Ogilvie got to his feet, glanced at Stuart, and then followed the ADC to the General's presence. Sir Clarence was seated at his desk beneath another portrait, that of Her Imperial Majesty the Queen-Empress, permanently staring down her nose at visitors to the Major-General Commanding her Southern Army in India. Ogilvie marched smartly towards the desk and stood at attention; this time, there was no invitation to be seated. Sir Clarence stared at .him, his face redder than ever between the snow-white whiskers.

"Ogilvie. A pretty kettle of fish, what?"

"Sir."

"Son of an old friend—I don't like it, damned if I do. Whatever possessed you?"

"I don't know, sir. I can only say I'm sorry, sir."

"So I should think. Anything else, any excuses?"

"No, sir."

"That's honest. Uniform?"

Ogilvie stared in some surprise. "Sir?"

"You've got yer uniform here, I take it—that is, in Coimbatore? Full dress uniform?"

"Yes, sir."

"Well, that's as I thought." Farrar-Drumm seemed much relieved. "That's one reason why the Court Martial had to be held here—take too long to muster everyone's kit and send it up to Secunderabad."

"I see, sir," Ogilvie said in some astonishment at an incongruous statement.

"And time's of the essence. That damn feller Rangapore seems to be everywhere according to the despatches, and I have to get yer Colonel back to his regiment." Farrar-Drumm cleared his throat with a rumble that ended in an attack of coughing. His face went almost purple. "Now, I'll say nothing about His Royal Highness at this stage. You're well enough aware of the implications, and no doubt aware of my own grief as well. I've taken yer Colonel's report, and

105

Brigadier-General Masefield's. That's the basis. One of my staff officers will see you presently, and inform you of the charges against you, you understand?"

"Yes, sir."

"You're entitled to prepare a defence, and an officer of the Judge Advocate-General's branch will be detailed to assist you, but time is short as I have said." Farrar-Drumm paused to blow his nose. "The Court Martial will assemble at ten o'clock tomorrow morning under my presidency. If you are surprised by my appointment, you should not be. In the circumstances—a royal personage—it's been considered proper that a General Officer should preside. Foreign courts and embassies . . . this is far from a usual case, and it'll go eventually before the Governor General in Council—the Viceroy, that is."

*   *   *

Ogilvie, given a room in the Staff quarters with a sentry posted outside, had time in which to reflect upon many things: firstly the fact that Sir Clarence had been remarkably mild in his manner and secondly that in strict military correctness the interview, since Farrar-Drumm was to preside at the Court Martial, should not have taken place at all. Either Sir Clarence was getting past command or there was an indication that leniency would be shown—there had been little actual censure through the short exchange. The intent could have been to reassure him, yet there had been reference to "the implications" and Ogilvie knew they were real enough, and could not be got round. After an hour's wait in his room, he was sent for, this time under Stuart's escort, to wait upon one Colonel Harwood of Farrar-Drum's staff. Harwood was very different from his master; small, dapper, with a clipped voice and a neat moustache forming the only facial hair, his manner was distant, formal and somehow menacing as he stated the charges: one, that Ogilvie had shown cowardice in not engaging the enemy,

106

thereby causing the death of His Royal Highness Prince George of Hohenzollern; two, that he had been guilty of failure to engage the enemy, this being the alternative charge should the first be thrown out by the Court Martial; three, that he had failed to press home an attack—yet another alternative; and four, that he had failed in his military duty to make a proper appreciation and reconnaissance of the position before entering the defile. After this interview Ogilvie was taken, still under escort, to another room where he had words with a major from the Judge Advocate-General's branch, who, as promised by the General, went into the question of the accused's defence. In full detail Ogilvie recounted the events of the night in question, while Major Bush listened carefully, interjecting a question now and again.

"Say as little as you can get away with, Ogilvie," Bush said after taking down his statement. "In my experience, most people manage to condemn themselves out of their own mouths. And don't get flustered— that's important."

"You mention people condemning themselves, Major. I take it you mean the guilty ones, whereas—"

"Whereas we're entering a plea of Not Guilty for you—yes, I know. But they almost all plead Not Guilty, Ogilvie." Bush tapped the sheet of paper before him. "You're going to be admitting, in effect, that you're guilty of the fourth charge, failure to assess, even though your plea is a blanket Not Guilty to them all. The verdict depends on what you say to the Court—or rather, what you *don't* say. So take my advice on that, old man. This statement's between you and me and will not be made available to the Court or the prosecution—"

"It's virtually what I reported to my Colonel and the General, Major."

Bush nodded. "Quite so, but that's another story. You'll be judged by the members of the Court, not by your earlier reports." He paused. "If you want my guess, you'll probably be found guilty on the fourth charge and acquitted on the

107

others—certainly you'll be acquitted on the first. I don't believe anyone's going to accuse you of cowardice. You did not in fact run away, and to stay is scarcely a coward's act."

"Then why include it in the charges?"

Bush pursed his mouth and blew out a long breath. "Damned if I know, really. Playing safe internationally . . . a Royal Highness is a Royal Highness, you know! Or . . ." He paused, looking hard at Ogilvie. "How d'you get on with your Colonel, or shouldn't I ask? As a fellow officer, I shouldn't, of course—but as your legal adviser, I suggest you answer frankly."

"Do you think he's responsible for that charge, then?"

"I've no idea," Bush said. "Just answer the question, if you please."

Ogilvie looked down at the desk, then up again at Bush. "He's a difficult man. Temperamental, autocratic, often sadistic. But by and large a good soldier, and certainly not one to avoid action, I would say."

"That's not quite what I asked, Ogilvie. How do you get on with him?"

"Badly," Ogilvie said after a pause. "We got off on the wrong foot from the start."

"You'd better eleborate. Discard all nagging worries about disloyalty! It's your future in the army that's at stake. Stick to the facts and there'll be no disloyalty. I've a feeling the facts are going to emerge in any case, and we don't want them slanted against you."

*   *   *

Another miserably sleepless night, dreading the morrow. Ogilvie had been frank with Bush regarding his relations with Lord Brora, and it had gone against the grain. One did not criticise one's Colonel outside the regiment; yet Ogilvie had been persuaded that he had a duty to be forthcoming, a duty to his brother officers and the other ranks, and also to his own family. The son of a serving General, a high-ranking officer such as Sir Iain, had to consider the facts of military life. It would not be fair to Sir Iain, Bush had said flatly, to hold back any possibly relevant facts. It still left a sour taste in the mouth. Ogilvie awoke to the cold of the Ootacamund morning feeling weary, and with a dull ache in his head, when a bearer came in with a jug of hot water. Breakfast was to be brought to his room; and Ogilvie washed and shaved carefully, eating the meal in his dressing-gown before putting on his full-dress uniform that had been brought up from the Coimbatore cantonment by an orderly the previous evening. By nine-thirty he was complete in green doublet, kilt, and white sporran with its three silver-mounted black tails, red and black diced stockings with the *skean dhu* thrust down the right leg, spats, and highly-polished black shoes. His feathered Highland bonnet with the flash of the Royal Strathspey lay ready on the table, beautifully smoothed by his allotted bearer. At nine-forty he was joined by Robin Stuart, also in his full-dress uniform. Little talk was exchanged; neither officer felt like it. His heart thumping, Ogilvie crossed the headquarters courtyard towards the chamber where the trial was to take place behind guarded doors. Walking into the room he found a number of persons already seated, officers from the garrison and a sprinkling of interested Civilians on leave from their government departments. Major Bush rose from behind a table and indicated where Ogilvie and Stuart were to sit; behind another table was Lord Brora with another of the Judge Advocate-General's officers. So far, the long green-baize-covered table at the end of the room was empty but for the Deputy Judge Advocate-General; soon it would be occupied by the members of the Court. As Ogilvie entered, there was a stir of interest: not so often was a Court Martial held on such charges as this. Insobriety was perhaps the worst that Ootacamund was accustomed to, or absence without leave, or plain disobedience of orders; the involvement of a royal prince was unique. In the front row of the public benches sat an elderly man bearing upon his face as much white hair as

Sir Clarence Farrar-Drumm, an important-looking man with cold eyes who sat staring ahead of him with arms folded across a black morning coat and a high starched collar biting deeply into overhanging jowls. Seeing the direction of Ogilvie's eye, Bush touched him on the shoulder and whispered, "Sir Henry Corke, representing the Viceroy."

"Quick work!"

"Fortuitously, he was here already."

"What'll he do?"

Bush said, "Nothing as regards the trial, of course. He's here purely to observe."

"And report."

"And report, as you say. Stop worrying, Ogilvie. It won't help you. I'm confident of the result even if you aren't."

"Suppose I'm acquitted on the first three charges, and found guilty on the fourth, as you suggested. What'll the sentence be, d'you think?"

Bush said impatiently, "We've considered that and I still don't know. If a prince wasn't involved I imagine you'd have got off with a reprimand, perhaps a loss of seniority at the most. But as it is . . ."

"Persons in high places have to have their honour satisfied!"

"Damn it all," Bush said wearily, "you've gone and trodden on the toes of the Queen-Empress herself to some extent! Now shut up and wait."

The wait seemed endless; but it was on the last stroke of ten o'clock that there was a stir in the room and the garrison Provost Marshal called upon all present to stand. Through a door to the left of the long table filed the members of the Court Martial: eight officers in full dress, one of them a lieutenant-colonel, the rest consisting of three majors and four captains. Remaining standing, they waited at their places while their President, Major-General Farrar-Drumm, entered and made his way slowly, limping a little from his rheumatics, to his place in their centre. He looked all round the courtroom, taking his time, looking resplendent in his

110

full-dress tunic of scarlet cloth, blue trousers with gold stripe, plumed cocked hat and crimson sash. Having taken his look, he nodded and said gravely, "Be seated, if you please, gentlemen."

"All sit," repeated the Provost Marshall, loudly. There was a rustle, a clank of spurs, and, from the long table, a shuffle of documents. The President formally started the proceedings, the accused was identified and the charges read by the Deputy Judge Advocate-General. The various allowed statements were read out to the Court, and then, after some loudly whispered consultation between Farrar-Drumm and the other officers, during which the Deputy Judge Advocate-General was consulted, Farrar-Drumm, who looked to Ogilvie somewhat uncertain, as though he were unfamiliar with Court Martial procedure, barked:

"Who comes to prosecute this officer, the accused?"

Brora rose to his feet. "I do, sir."

"And you are? I know who you are, of course, but I must be told formally, doncher know."

"Quite, sir. I am Major Lord Brora, acting Commanding Officer of the 2nd Battalion, the 114th Highlanders, the Queen's Own Royal Strathspeys."

"Acting Lieutenant-Colonel?"

"No, sir. I retain my rank of major, in fact, but as I said, I'm—"

"Yes, yes, all right. The 114th Highlanders being the accused's regiment?"

"Yes, sir."

"Then you are the accused's Commanding Officer, why the devil didn't you say so."

"You didn't ask, sir," Lord Brora said tartly.

"Kindly do not be impertinent to me, sir, or you will be in contempt of this court. I *did* ask. This is a very important matter, and it is very important that all the facts be clearly stated from the start." Farrar-Drumm turned to his neighbour. "What's next?" he asked in an audible whisper.

Ogilvie failed to hear the answer, but saw the looks on the

111

faces of the members of the Court; and saw the impotent impatience in Lord Brora's face, his fuming, his obvious desire to instruct Farrar-Drumm in proper procedure. The Deputy Judge Advocate-General, too, was looking put out and worried. There was some further delay and then once again Farrar-Drumm addressed Brora.

"As prosecuting officer, you will state yer case, Lord Brora."

"Very good, sir." Brora, still upon his feet, read from a prepared document, putting the bald facts of the night probe as ordered by the Brigadier-General and commanded by the accused—and, Ogilvie noted—putting them and his own subsequent report of events fairly and without bias. These facts put, the defence was invited to state its reply to the charges, and Bush rose to his duty, only to be halted by Farrar-Drumm.

"Damn it all, you're not the accused, are you?"

"No, sir. I represent the defence, as the detailed officer of the Judge Advocate-General's branch."

"Oh, I see. Very well, then, kindly proceed, whoever you are."

"Major Bush, sir. Thank you, sir." Bush proceeded, stating Ogilvie's case as baldly as Brora had stated his; Farrar-Drumm appeared not to be listening, sitting with his head in his hands and his eyes apparently shut. When Bush reached the end of his statement, however, the President's eyes opened and once again he addressed Brora.

"Lord Brora, have you any questions you wish to ask the accused, and have you witnesses to substantiate yer charges as made?"

"Yes to both your questions, sir."

"Then the witnesses first, I think."

"Very good, sir. I call Bruce Andrew Fraser, lieutenant in the 114th Highlanders."

The call was repeated, and Fraser, in full dress like the other military officers, rose and proceeded to the witness stand. In answer to Lord Brora's questions he established his identity and agreed the facts as given by his acting Colonel, confirming that he had been Ogilvie's second-in-command and had not been aware of any order to open fire, though he added that he had not been present in the defile or at the attack. The other witnesses followed him, the next being Sergeant Davison, whose testimony was interrupted by the President. "Lord Brora, you are merely establishing the established. The accused has never denied that he didn't open fire, has he?"

"No, sir, but—"

"Then kindly try to shorten the proceedings, we haven't got all day."

Brora lowered his sheaf of papers and banged them against his kilted thigh. "With the greatest respect, sir, it is my right to have my witnesses utter. May I proceed?"

Farrar-Drumm lifted his eyebrows. "Deputy Judge Advocate-General?"

"The prosecution is in order, sir."

"Oh, very well, then. But do have an eye to the clock." Farrar-Drumm paused. "Tell me, Lord Brora, what do you propose to attempt to establish next?"

"Amongst other matters, sir, I am attempting to establish the vital *importance* of these proceedings, which you yourself have—"

"I have warned you once before about impertinence of tone, Lord Brora. I shall not warn you a third time, you may be sure. Kindly confine yerself to answering my questions. I shall ask the last one again: what, pray, will you attempt to establish next?"

"I am leading up, sir, to the nub of my charges against Captain Ogilvie, and I am establishing a pattern of behaviour, as will emerge under cross examination." Brora, once again lowering his sheaf of notes, stared arrogantly at the members of the Court Martial. "I shall now carry on with my questions to my witnesses, with your leave, gentlemen." Farrar-Drumm shrugged, looking thoroughly put out and aggrieved, but no further objections were raised and the proceedings continued, the two *jemadars* following separately to the witness stand. Ogilvie listened closely, while Major Bush made detailed notes. The answers given by the various witnesses appeared innocuous enough and Ogilvie remarked as much in a whisper to Bush.

"Possibly," Bush said non-committally.

"Why only possibly?"

"As your Colonel said earlier, he's establishing a pattern. We just have to wait and see."

Ogilvie nodded and said no more. The business dragged on; now all the members of the Court were becoming restive, and Brora seemed to sense this. Dismissing the last of his witnesses he said abruptly, "Thank you, gentlemen, for your forbearance. I should now like to ask some questions of the accused."

Farrar-Drumm nodded his consent. Bush whispered, "Careful of your tongue, remember what I said," and Ogilvie got up and walked to the witness stand, his mouth dry. The routine questions as to identity and regiment were gone through, and then, as Brora opened his attack, the atmosphere in the court changed abruptly and dramatically.

Drawing himself to his full height, looking magnificent and formidable in his green doublet and badges of rank, Lord Brora said calmly, "I shall now show the Court that the accused is a squeamish officer with no stomach for action, and that on the night when these sad events took place, his dislike of gunfire led to the supreme military crime of cowardice."

There was a hush; Ogilvie, caught off guard, looked across at Bush for guidance. Bush, his expression grim, rose to his feet and addressed Farrar-Drumm. "Sir, I must protest—"

"At what, Major Bush? The charge sheet includes the accusation of cowardice, does it not?"

"It does, sir, but—"

"No buts, Major Bush." Farrar-Drumm had suddenly become much more incisive. "The prosecution is entitled to attempt to prove its case. Lord Brora, you may proceed."

Nine

As he started his questioning, there appeared to be no passion in Lord Brora. He was cool, calculating and spoke calmly, almost conversationally. "Captain Ogilvie, I ask you to be good enough to cast your mind back. Do you understand me?"

"I think I do, sir." Ogilvie had been advised that in court he should employ the more usual "sir" in place of the regimental mode of address.

"Good. You will recall the detraining of the brigade at Coimbatore railway station on 14th January?"

"Yes, sir."

Brora stared straight at Ogilvie. "Tell the Court, if you please, what occurred."

"There was some trouble with the natives, sir."

"Yes. There was an attack—"

"Not an attack, sir. A hostile movement, yes."

Brora lost some of his calm. He snapped, "Kindly don't argue with me, Captain Ogilvie. What else is a hostile movement but an attack? You play with words. There was an attack, I say. An attack. You were the officer most immediately involved, were you not?"

"I was, sir."

"Thank you. You were ordered by me personally to open fire upon the mob. My precise words were . . ." Lord Brora looked down and read from his notes. "I said, you'll open upon them at once. Did I not say that, Captain Ogilvie?"

Ogilvie answered stiffly. "Yes, sir."

"And did you open fire?"

"Sir, I gave the order—"

"I repeat, did you open fire, or did you refuse to obey my order? Kindly answer the question, Captain Ogilvie."

Ogilvie glanced first at Bush, then at the Deputy Judge Advocate-General, then at Farrar-Drumm: he found no help in their faces, though Bush appeared to be trying as it were to will something into his mind. He licked his lips and said, "I did not open fire on the natives, sir, but—"

"Then you refused to obey my order."

"I gave the order to fire over their heads, sir."

Brora shrugged. "The point is made and there is no more to be said. My order was not obeyed, and I ask the Court to take note, if it please them."

From the long table Farrar-Drumm said, "Note will be taken, Lord Brora, but I should point out that I was myself present upon that occasion. I considered the whole brigade to be taken unawares, not just Captain Ogilvie. I also noted that you were carrying a *syce* confined in a cage—and if my memory serves me well, I think I expressed my disapproval, did I not?"

Brora glared. "That is scarcely an issue in this case, sir, and I protest at your remark."

"Oh, you do, do you? Let me remind you, I'm the President of this Court and I shall remark as I think fit—" Farrar-Drumm broke off as he saw the hasty signal from the Deputy Judge Advocate-General, who bent across the intervening officers and whispered at some length. The officer of the legal branch had a despairing look on his face, had indeed worn it for some time, as though all his interjections were doomed to be waved irritably away by Farrar-Drumm. However, he achieved some success: the General cleared his throat and said, looking put out, "Oh, very well, very well, have it yer own way. I withdraw my remark. Go on, Lord Brora."

There was a smirk on Brora's face, and he gave an ironic bow towards Farrar-Drumm. "Thank you, sir." He turned back to Ogilvie. "Another excursion into the recent past. Were you not the officer in command of an escort to march a

116

man to the civil jail in Coimbatore from the regiment's cantonment on the day following our arrival there?"

Ogilvie nodded. "I was."

"And did you not meet trouble along the route, from a hostile mob?"

"There was some—"

"Yes, or no, Captain Ogilvie."

"In that case, sir—yes."

"Thank you. You and your men were assailed by flung stones and dirt, and there was some bloodshed—"

"Only from a stone—"

"I have warned you before about interrupting, Captain Ogilvie, and I have no doubt the Court is taking due note of your rude and arrogant behaviour. There was an attack, and blood was drawn. Now you shall tell the Court what my prior order was, given only moments before you took out the escort. Well?"

"You spoke of opening fire, sir."

"Spoke of opening fire!" Lord Brora repeated in a scathing tone. "My dear sir, my order was quite precise. I told you you would not hesitate to shoot, that you were to use your rifles against any attempt to prevent the man's jail delivery taking place. You asked, indeed, if that was to be considered an order, and I replied that it certainly was. Do you deny this?"

"No, sir."

"I am glad to hear it," Brora said tartly.

"And you also said, sir—"

"I am not interested in what else I said, Captain Ogilvie, and you will—"

"One moment, Lord Brora." This was Farrar-Drumm. "Yes, Major Bush, I see that you wish to protest and I shall uphold you. Lord Brora, the Court will wish to hear what else you said." He paused. "The accused may proceed."

"Thank you, sir," Ogilvie said gratefully. To Brora he said, "You expressly told me not to fail to distinguish between a deliberate attack and pure mob harassment, sir."

117

"Another play upon words, Captain Ogilvie, a practice at which you are very adept I must say—"

'And in my judgement, sir, there was harassment rather than attack."

"Then you admit you didn't open fire?"

Ogilvie flushed at the way he had walked into a trap, none the less effective for its being fortuitous on Brora's part. "I admit that, yes."

"Then you failed to obey my order. And you say you considered the mob's conduct to fall within the definition of simple harassment?"

"Yes, sir—"

"Then why, pray tell me, did the governor of the jail see fit to send the cavalry to your assistance? I understand that a squadron of lancers and a battery of horse artillery were needed to do the job you had failed to do yourself. Can you perhaps explain this, Captain Ogilvie?"

Ogilvie floundered; he was a poor hand at this sort of self-justification. It was the man on the spot who had to make the instant decisions, and afterwards it was often hard to sort out one's motives, one's sequence of thought and assessment. He tried to express the truth, the facts as they had seemed to him at the time, that to have opened fire would have been only to precipitate a massacre of his men. Lord Brora, pouncing, made much of this: battle was a soldier's *raison d'être,* lethal risk his natural lot, death his glorious accolade. The Raj had not been won by namby-pambyism, nor would it be held by the same. When the adjournment for luncheon came, Ogilvie felt the day was lost for him.

*   *   *

"It's plain what he's after," Bush said. "In fact he came out with it openly enough, didn't he?"

"To prove I've always been a coward?"

"Bluntly, yes—in his experience, that is. Your past record stands, you know."

118

"But will it count?"

"It should," Bush said energetically, 'and I think it will, though perhaps only in mitigation if you understand me."

"You mean it won't help the actual verdict?"

"Not necessarily, but we shall see, we shall see. It's not going all in Brora's favour, you know! I was watching the faces behind the table when he went on about death's accolade and all that—the younger ones, anyway. The army's changing, Ogilvie, and leaving the Farrar-Drumms behind. The Broras too—he's really an anachronism. Death may still be the accolade, perhaps, but we don't chuck lives away *quite* so blithely as we used to!" Bush made an expansive gesture with his arms. "What's the use of a slaughtered escort, for God's sake? There's more common-sense and practicality around today."

"You mean—"

"I mean this, Ogilvie: I saw some of those faces registering that it was no bad thing for an officer to have a reasonable care for his men's lives. And the antithesis: that officers like the good Lord Brora are too damn blood-thirsty to hold command in India as it's become latterly. I won't attempt to prophesy, but he could find himself hoist with his own petard if he's not a little more careful."

*   *   *

The sitting was resumed; the proceedings opened more quietly after luncheon, with Farrar-Drumm showing signs of a fair amount of brandy taken with the rich meal. It was now the turn of the defence, and Bush was attempting to demolish the case built up by the prosecution, stressing Ogilvie's prudent withholding of fire in the incidents referred to by his acting Colonel, stressing the very great difference between the conduct of the regiment by Lord Dornoch and Lord Brora, and suggesting that the more humane outlook and more compassionate methods of the former had conditioned the officers to a different response and, overall, a wiser one. Proceeding on towards the events of the relevant night, Bush made his points firmly: the battalion was on exercises, Ogilvie had been ordered out on exercise against friendly troops, there was nothing to suggest that actual enemy forces would be encountered, and the native levies such as those of the Nizam of Hyderabad were notorious for using their weapons when they should not; they were basically wild men, with a code of discipline, if such existed at all, very different from that of the men of the British and Indian Armies under their white officers. Ogilvie's action in not returning the fire had been perhaps unfortunate; but it had been natural and in its way proper: if the affair had been as he had in genuine fact supposed—if the men upon the heights above the defile had been the Nizam's troops—what would have been the result of opening upon them and killing them? The whole of Central India might well have gone up in flames and in slaughter of the innocents. The Raj, Bush said firmly, should think itself lucky that it was Ogilvie who had commanded the probe and not some injudicious hothead. "If such had been the case—"

"*If,*" Brora said loudly.

Farrar-Drumm looked up, face shielded by a blue-veined hand. "What was that?"

Brora stood, tall and dominant. "I said *if*, sir. The defence is based upon an *if*. The prosecution is not. We are here to talk about what happened, not what might have happened but didn't. The defence has suggested that there was nothing to indicate that actual enemy forces might be about. *I* submit that I said to the accused, my very words, that all personnel were to be armed with live ammunition, just in case of bandits, and—"

"Bandits, sir, as you say," Bush interjected, rising to his feet. "Not rebel forces."

"You play with words like the accused, I think," Brora snapped.

"Is it not the fact that the rebels were not expected so far north, sir?"

"Trouble is *always* to be expected in India. Captain Ogilvie knew very well that the idea was to have British troops in the area simply *because* trouble was expected." Lord Brora turned upon the members of the Court. "May I remind you, gentlemen, that the Raj has no reason to think itself lucky as the defence suggests, nor has His Royal Highness, his *late* Royal Highness, Prince George of Hohenzollern. He is dead."

Brora sat down, looking about himself triumphantly. Farrar-Drumm said, "Very well, yer point is taken. Major Bush, you must confine yerself to the facts."

"Yes, sir. I'm sorry. But it is the facts upon which any officer has to make his appreciations—the facts *as believed by that officer*. There can be no other basis." Bush paused. "The defence is ready to admit a possible error of judgment, of assessment, but no more—and insists that the appreciation as made was the only one it was possible or prudent to make at that time. I suggest—" His sentence was rudely interrupted: a loud knock had come on the guarded door of the courtroom, and as Farrar-Drumm glared towards the sound the door opened and one of the sentries appeared, followed closely by an infantry major.

Farrar-Drumm's white eyebrows rose. "What's this?" he demanded crossly of the intruder. "Do you not know, my dear sir, that a Court Martial is in progress?"

"Yes, sir. I apologise, sir, but the matter is most urgent—"

"Then kindly state it without further ado, and then go away."

"Sir, the matter is for your ears only in the first instance." The officer stared pointedly at the Civilians in the body of the courtroom. "A strictly military matter at this stage, sir."

"Oh. Oh, very well, approach the table then, and tell me."

"Sir!" The Major came forward with his Wolseley helmet beneath his left arm. Halting smartly before the General, he bent to speak privately. The effect was immediate and electric.

Loudly Farrar-Drumm said, "Good God! You're sure?"

The officer bent again. "I see. Then you did quite right to interrupt, Major. You must return to yer unit at once." He rose to his feet, stared along the table, his face working, then turned to the body of the Court. "The case is adjourned *sine die*. All persons not concerned are to leave the room instantly. Be about yer business, if you please." As the surprised spectators began to file out, the General remained standing. When the last had gone—all, that was, except for the representative of His Excellency the Viceroy—and the doors had been closed behind them, Farrar-Drumm addressed the members of the Court. "There is news of war, gentlemen, of rebellion. The Rajah of Rangapore has risen against the Nizam and has attacked along the railway line running from Mormugao to Madras, in the region of Koppal. He has thrown in massive forces and has taken Koppal, Bellary and Guntakal, and is believed to be about to thrust north towards the Kistna River." He paused, breathing hard. "All officers are ordered to rejoin their units immediately, including those from the 114th Highlanders."

*   *   *

The order was not to apply to Ogilvie: the Viceroy's man, Sir Henry Corke, protested firstly that a vital case had been interrupted with no date set for re-convening the Court, and secondly that the President should not for one moment consider returning the accused to his regiment in the absence of a verdict. Farrar-Drumm was short with the first complaint, but gave in on the second: Ogilvie was ordered to remain in arrest and be escorted down to the Coimbatore garrison to await further orders.

Farrar-Drumm was apologetic. "I'm sorry—I understand yer wish to be with yer men—but there it is." He looked across at Robin Stuart. "You must rejoin, of course, with the others from yer regiment. My Provost Marshal will provide an escort from his corps. You'll remain only until relieved, Captain what's-yer-name." Current matters thus decided, Sir

Clarence left the room, leaning upon the arm of an ADC, to proceed about his duty of succouring the Raj and the Nizam of Hyderabad. With Stuart, Ogilvie went back to his quarters. Stuart was sympathetic and understanding enough, but only too obviously anxious to be northbound to rejoin the march on the Kistna River from Secunderabad. Soon after they reached Ogilvie's room an officer of captain's rank knocked to introduce himself: one Nesbitt, detailed by the Provost Marshal as personal escort for the accused. This officer added that the mountain railway would take all the 114th's personnel down to Coimbatore in an hour's time and that a connection for the town of Yadgir would be waiting for them all except Ogilvie who would remain as ordered in Coimbatore. At Yadgir arrangements would be made for horses to be in readiness to ride the others straight to where the battalion was understood to be on the march, not in fact a very great distance from the town.

*   *   *

In his allotted quarter in garrison, Ogilvie walked up and down, seething, frustrated, while Captain Nesbitt, a stolid man, played patience with two travelling-size packs of cards. Nesbitt was monosyllabic and policemanlike, an unimaginative man promoted from the ranks on transfer to provost duties from the Lincolnshire Regiment. He was also a gloomy man, given to much head-shaking and lip-pursing and could offer Ogilvie no promise of a speedy end to his ordeal. But later in the day, after Lord Brora and his witnesses had departed in the train for Yadgir, fresh orders came: Sir Henry Corke had been in communication with Calcutta by means of the telegraph, and word had come through that Captain Ogilvie was, in the very special circumstances, to be despatched by train to the capital, still under arrest, and would be interviewed by the Viceregal staff so that urgent questions from Whitehall could be met.

"Irregular, isn't it?" Ogilvie asked.

"I don't know about that."

"In the middle of a Court Martial?"

"Well, yes, there's that." Captain Nesbitt sadly pulled at his drooping moustache. "But then, you see, a *royal* gentleman's involved, and a German at that. When royalty gets involved, well, there's no knowing what procedures may go by the board. An' all we 'ave to do is to obey orders."

"Quite," Ogilvie said shortly. "Well, when do we leave?"

Nesbitt shuffled his cards and said, "His Excellency wants you urgent an' a special train's being laid on. One coach, with clearance through for Calcutta, an' leaves at six pip emma."

Ten

THE STEAMY ENGINE with its single coach carried a crew of driver and fireman and guard, plus a commissariat staff of Indians to attend upon the needs of the two officers. Ogilvie sat in state with Captain Nesbitt, who once again brought out his playing-cards as the coach was pulled away from Coimbatore for its long haul north. In the guard's van sat a sergeant and four lance-corporals from the Provost Marshal's department, as aides to Captain Nesbitt and also to act as the train's defence should bandits be encountered en route. Ogilvie felt desperate depression creep over him as the coach creaked along in a cloud of steam and smoke and Captain Nesbitt carefully studied his cards, which Ogilvie would dearly have loved to scoop up and chuck from the window so that the man would be forced to make some kind of conversation. Night came down and lamps were lit; a meal was brought, and Nesbitt put aside his cards to eat, an exercise which also, it seemed, precluded conversation. Dinner over, cards were resumed: for the umpteenth time Captain Nesbitt turned aside a suggestion that they might play something two-handed.

"I only play patience, Captain Ogilvie, nothing else. I'm a self-contained kind o' person. So was my old father. As a matter o' fact, 'e was playing patience right at the time o' death."

"I'm sorry—"

"It was 'is way."

"Was he in the army too?"

"Yes. Sar'nt-Major o' the Sherwood Foresters. Pegged out in Wigan, where 'e was living at the time." Captain Nesbitt returned to his solitary game. The night wore on; at ten-thirty Ogilvie, closely attended by Nesbitt, went to the sleeping compartment and turned in while a bearer folded his full-dress uniform: as a result of one of the quirks of military life, this time some malfunction on the part of the transport authority, Ogilvie's gear had been sent up the line for onward freight to Calcutta in the train that had taken Brora and the witnesses to Yadgir, and on his return from Ootacamund he had been unable to change out of his full dress regalia. He found little sleep that night; there was much shunting and whistling at a junction, and some time spent in a siding, then the train chuffed on through the Nilgiri Hills. Unable to remain any longer in his bunk, Ogilvie got up almost with the dawn, and so, hearing his movement, did Nesbitt, a conscientious man. Ogilvie was bleary-eyed and ill-tempered. Soon after an early breakfast had been cleared away, Captain Nesbitt brought out his cards; and towards noon the train ground to a halt amid much steam and shouting from the crew. Nesbitt left his game and thrust his head from the window: he had a fair knowledge of the local dialect and was able to inform Ogilvie that there was a mechanical breakdown, which might well take some hours to repair.

"Can they do it on their own?"

"They think so, yes. And they tell me we're still well south of Nanjangud, which itself is south of Mysore."

"We've not made much progress, then."

"No."

The card-playing was resumed and Ogilvie was unable to contain himself. "Don't you," he asked, *"ever* do anything at all but play patience, Nesbitt?"

"Pardon?" There was a hurt look from above the walrus-like moustache. "That was uncalled-for, Captain Ogilvie, very uncalled-for in my opinion—"

"I'm sorry."

"Granted. I do my duty, and I 'ope pleasantly and without rancour?"

126

"Yes, of course you do—"

"An' I'm partial to a game o' patience to pass the time."

Ogilvie subsided and sank back into his seat, biting his finger-nails. The heat was stifling; from outside came a deluge of shouting and clanging which to some extent was soaked up by the thick deciduous forest that clad the slopes of the Nilgiris; now and then, when the sounds of a difficult repair were temporarily stilled, bird cries came. The afternoon dragged on towards another nightfall, and the night birds replaced those of daylight, among them the blue-necked bee-eater remarkable for its short, harsh, grating voice. Still the work continued, now under flares and lanterns. Before the light went, a hand-propelled truck had come down upon them from the station at Nanjangud, carrying chattering natives to enquire why the train had not yet come through. After some bad-tempered altercation with the engine-driver, the truck was propelled back to base and a query was left in the air as to whether or not it would come back with a full repair gang. Just before dinner was due to be served to the two British officer sahibs, and while, once again, Captain Nesbitt was playing patience, there was a disturbance on the track outside, some excited velling, and then sudden rifle fire. Alongside Ogilvie .e window shattered: he felt the graze of the bullet that struck and killed Nesbitt. Nesbitt, taken through the head, fell forward and then lay still, blood pouring over the table that stood between them. Ogilvie dived for cover beneath the table, looked up at Nesbitt's lifeless legs. Like father, like son: they had both died whilst playing patience.

*   *   *

With the exception of Ogilvie himself, the bandits had made a clean sweep. The train crew had been mown down in the first volley, and lay dead beside the track—guard, engine-driver and fireman. The kitchen staff lay huddled in death in their pantry compartment. Ogilvie had joined the sergeant and his lance-corporals in the guard's van and they had fought back strongly: many bandits had fallen. Ogilvie, leaping down from the van under covering fire from the provost section, hurled himself on two of the bandits; they dodged, and his impetus carried him into the trees and into contact with a hard trunk that knocked him cold. Recovering consciousness, he saw the colandered bodies of the sergeant and the rest, some hanging from the door of the guard's van, some upon the track. He searched around for the revolver he had taken from Nesbitt's body: there was no sign of it in the thick forest undergrowth. From the train came sounds of plunder. Disarmed, and on his own, he had the one course left: to abandon a train he could not conceivably defend—there was, in any case, nothing left to defend other than a coach and a broken-down engine. He moved back, unseen as the bandits concentrated upon their booty, moved into the cover of the forest, lying low when he was far enough away. Some fifteen minutes later sounds of departure came, and then there was silence; the bandits had made their escape into the forest on the other side of the railway line. Ogilvie waited a while then moved back towards the track and climbed aboard the coach. The bodies had all been left where they had died and the rifles had been taken: to steal arms may well have been the purpose of the attack. Ogilvie looked around: other things had gone too. In the van were a number of trunks and articles of furniture belonging to officers moved up from the Coimbatore garrison, put aboard for transport to stations north. The trunks had been burst open and ransacked, and anything of value would have now been taken, but a good deal of rumpled clothing remained: the bandits would no doubt have seen a risk in being found with the clothing of British sahibs.

Ogilvie took stock of his situation: he knew from Nesbitt that he was as yet well south of Mysore, with virtually all his journey to Calcutta still before him. It was likely enough, indeed it could be regarded as certain, that the hand-truck from Nanjangud would return by morning at the latest, and it

128

was undoubtedly his duty to await it and then ask for transport to the nearest military camp or cantonment. He was still under arrest, though without an escort . . . and the lack of an escort made no difference to his duty: his duty, as an officer in arrest, was to surrender his person the soonest possible. Of that there could be no doubt at all.

But his regiment was not all that far to the north.

*   *   *

There was a suit of fine light-brown cloth: the fit was hazardous but would have to do; Ogilvie took off his uniform. Round the starched upright collar of his full-dress shirt he tied a cravat adapted from his own large silk handkerchief. He retained his own black uniform shoes since no civilian pairs fitted. The rest of his uniform he bundled into a Gladstone bag that had been emptied by the bandits, its lock broken open. Then he dropped down once again to the track. The suit was uncomfortable, constricting him under his armpits, and the trousers failed to reach his ankles adequately, and there was no hat: but he would be far less conspicuous than if he were wearing his uniform. Losing no time he struck out in the direction of Nanjangud, following the track but keeping in the forest's cover. He kept going all through the night, slept a while on the fringe of the forest as he began to approach the plain, wakened to hear movement on the track, an engine making for the breakdown at last. He slept a while longer then moved on, crossing the railway line to head north-westerly when he saw distantly the clustered buildings around the halt of Nanjangud. He kept well clear of the town. Once away from Nanjangud, and unseen, he came to a river, and began a search for a ford; by the ford when he found it during the afternoon there was a small town with a market-place and he decided he had now to take a risk, for he could go little farther north without food and transport. He had enough rupees on him provided he could bargain satisfactorily; and the fact that he was a hatless sahib, wearing an ill-fitting suit and carrying a Gladstone bag without a coolie to do it for him, did not seem to register with the good natives of the town. All sahibs were mad and in India grew worse; and all sahibs grew very much madder if interfered with, or questioned, or stared at—and sahibs were very powerful, never to be angered except perhaps by a mob when deep passions had been aroused, which was a totally different matter. And sahibs had money; this sahib, as it appeared, being no exception. Ogilvie was able to purchase a hat from a market stall dealing in cast-off garments, also a more comfortable and civilian-looking shirt, and a voluminous cloak of a thick tweed that would keep out the cold of the nights. And last but most important to him currently, a seedy horse was obtained from something like a knacker's yard for the expenditure of many rupees, with adequate harness and saddle supplied along with the beast itself. In final addition to his equipage he purchased a carpet-bag and filled it with what he regarded as iron rations: bread that while it would grow stale over the days ahead would be sustaining, fruit, chocolate and some tins of bully beef clearly stolen from some British commissariat store. Topping all this with a water-bottle he rode out of the little town, crossed the ford, and headed north along a track that would lead him, he believed, eventually towards the Kistna River and the fighting. Farther than this he did not as yet commit his plans: actually to rejoin his regiment under Lord Brora would doubtless be unwise to say the least, but it should prove possible to attach himself to some other unit in the area when in the heat and necessities of action perhaps not too many questions would be asked of a willing reinforcement. But as the time passed, and he rode or rested himself and his mount, or ate, he became more and more aware of his precarious position. He had acted in haste in the first place, rashly, and God alone could now tell what the consequences might be. Old Farrar-Drumm would be livid and would be assailed for losing an important prisoner from his command, assailed from all sides—the Queen-Empress,

Whitehall, the Viceroy, the Governor of Madras and the Commander-in-Chief. His wrath would fall like that of the Almighty. Ogilvie's one defence would be that he had run towards action and not from it . . . with a heart that now seemed to sink with every hoofbeat of his lonely northward advance, but with a deep determination nevertheless since the die was cast, Ogilvie rode on like a landbound homing pigeon, mapless, without a compass, using the sun as his guide, replenishing his water-stocks as and where he could, allowing his horse to munch where and what it could find as the plain temperatures boiled by day and at night came close to freezing him.

* * *

"A damn fine time of it Ogilvie's given us!" Lord Brora, reaching the end of his ride out of Yadgir, reined in his horse for a moment as he saw the extended picquets of the regiment ahead, below distant rising ground and beyond patches of scrubby bush. He was in a vile temper; the journey had been hasty and uncomfortable, with none of the ordinary civilities of life laid on. From time to time at the en route railway stations word sent by the telegraph had awaited the acting Colonel of the Royal Strathspey, word that the Rangapore hordes were moving swiftly on the Kistna. Other news had come also, news that accounted for much of the vileness of Brora's mood, news that he imparted to Andrew Black when the Adjutant came riding up to welcome him back.

"We're glad to see you, sir." Black's expression gave the lie to his words: he disliked handing back the command.

Brora returned Black's salute ill-temperedly. "Be that as it may, Captain Black. I have had tidings."

"Of the enemy, sir?"

"Not entirely of the enemy, no. Of Ogilvie." Brora, in his loud voice, gave Black the details of the interrupted proceedings and of Ogilvie's later disappearance. His face was

131

livid. "An engine and coach—his—found with dead aboard, and ransacked. No Ogilvie. Either he's been taken by bandits, or he cut and run. Would you believe it! Farrar-Drumm's as damn senile as my maiden aunt, not to have put the fellow in irons!"

Black was gaping from horseback. "My God! Nothing further known, sir?"

"Nothing. Damnable fellow! Run before he could be involved in action, I've no doubt!"

Black pursed his lips. Brora went on in his harsh voice, "I shall now report to the Brigadier-General, and after that you'll parade the battalion in hollow square about me. I shall have words with the men."

Brora touched his spurs lightly to his horse's flanks and rode on, his head held back haughtily, his left hand resting on his thigh. When the mounted party reached the battalion, fallen out to rest and to allow its Colonel to rejoin and make his reports to Brigade, the word spread like wildfire that Captain Ogilvie was missing from Southern Army Headquarters. There was much speculation, but none of it was of a dishonourable nature: James Ogilvie's courage was well enough known and there was plenty of sympathy for him in the Scots ranks. When word reached the Regimental Sergeant-Major via Colour-Sergeant MacTrease, Cunningham rose and fell for a while on the balls of his feet, saying nothing.

"What d'ye think he's done, Sar'nt-Major?"

"Think, Colour? I don't think, man, I know! Captain Ogilvie's for the fight, o' course! What else did you imagine?"

"Nothing else. I'm with you. The question is, how and where?"

Cunningham gave a hard laugh, a vindictive one for a man who was never vindictive. "Wherever he can take a pot shot at bloody Brora—or that's what I'd do in Captain Ogilvie's shoes!" He sucked in his breath, and stared at MacTrease. "And that's between you and me and the tent-peg, Mac. A word out of place and so help me God I'll have your guts."

MacTrease grinned. "I reckon I'm safe. I feel the same way myself, and so do many of the lads out there."

Cunningham gave him a bleak look. "Do you mean that literally?"

"Officers have been shot in the back before now, Sar'nt-Major."

"I know! Not in the 114th, though. And never will be. If you've any doubts at all, Colour MacTrease, you'll watch it. Never heed my remarks just now." Cunningham prodded the Colour-Sergeant in the chest with his pace-stick. "You'll watch it like a bloody hawk. That's not the way it must be."

"Aye, sir, I'll watch it," MacTrease said. He stiffened to respectful attention, then marched away towards B Company, thinking of his officer. Ogilvie was all right in his view, and "all right" spoke volumes. Brora was a bastard, and bastards got, in the end, what they deserved. Very often they did in fact get it in action, and Scots soldiers were as hard as nails, a very different proposition from any English battalion yet known to God or man. Justifiable homicide, call it murder if you wanted, was all the same as killing the enemy—or could be so considered if a man was sufficiently stirred in his mind, and there were occasions when even a Colour-Sergeant could nod, and see bugger-all. MacTrease very devoutly wished Ogilvie well, and mentally damned his acting Colonel to the everlasting fires reserved for bastards. He went meanwhile about his duties and within the next half-hour the bugles sounded down the resting line for the battalion to fall in. Verbal orders were passed from the Adjutant and RSM for the men to form about the Colonel; and into the hollow square Lord Brora rode, tweaking at his moustache, his eyes hard and disdainful.

"You men." The voice was like the impact of a bullet. "You already know you're marching into action, real action, and now I'm back with you it won't be long before we reach the scene. I'm authorised to tell you that the rebel forces of the Rajah of Rangapore are advancing north from below the

133

Tunga Bhadra River, upon which they have their picquets, towards the Kistna. Their intention is probably to straddle the Kistna, consolidate, and advance north through the central plain to take Hyderabad. That's *their* intention. *Mine* is to stop them. I expect to bring them to action at first light the day after tomorrow, when we shall find ourselves not far off the Kistna River. Other battalions, other British formations, will also be seeking the honour of bringing them to a halt. I intend to get there first. I take it that's understood." He paused. "Captain Black?"

Black saluted from horseback. "Sir!"

"The battalion's to be pushed hard, without mercy. I want to cover a wide front. Therefore you shall detail enough scouts and picquets to extend me as far as is humanly possible, and instant reports are to be made of the first sighting of the enemy. Understood, Captain Black?"

"Yes, sir."

"See to it, then." Brora lifted his body, standing in his stirrups. "God help any man who fails to do his duty. God help any man who does less than his best. God help any man who turns his back. If God doesn't help you, you may rely upon it *I* shall not. Captain Black?"

"Sir!"

"March the regiment out as soon as the bugle sounds from Brigade." Brora swung his horse round and rode out of the square. Apart from the sound of the hooves there was a dead silence. The faces of the men were a study: they were never slow in action, afraid inside themselves as often they might be; there was not a man among them that did not resent their Colonel's ranting tone and insulting words. And, incredibly, into that total silence fell one single voice, calling out in a great, angry yell:

"Three cheers, lads, for Captain Ogilvie!"

Black, following behind Lord Brora, turned his horse, his dark face seeming suddenly drained of blood. Ahead of him the Colonel halted. Then the cheering broke out, loud, angry, menacing, wave upon wave, far more than three, and was followed by a low but rising murmur of hatred. Black started shouting and riding forward, but his voice was unheard. The sergeants and colour-sergeants were shouting with the rest; only the Regimental Sergeant-Major was standing silent, but it was plain where his feelings lay: his face was working with emotion and he was making no effort to still the racket. As Black sat his horse looking hopeless, uncertain and beaten, Lord Brora was seen to continue his ride away, not once having looked back. He rode straight, head high as ever, every line, every movement of his body expressing contempt and arrogance and disdain. It was a curious moment; the noise began to die away, slow at first then faster, until once again there was silence. Men exchanged glances; no order was given. The Adjutant still seemed paralysed. Under their own volition the ranks broke up, the men falling out from the square to assemble raggedly by companies to await the blowing of the Brigade bugles. Cunningham came to life and marched down the line, shoulders back, left-right-left, shouting the men into column and putting distance between himself and the Adjutant. Nothing was said about the incident; within minutes the strident notes of the bugles sounded out over the lonely plain beneath a high sun, and the men marched away under the colour-sergeants whose crimson sashes seemed a fitting emblem, an earnest of the blood that lay ahead; imaginations winged towards the south where the clustering vultures, as though word had reached them, might well be sharpening their beaks in anticipation.

Eleven

OGILVIE WAS BY now dog tired, so was his horse. The two of
them moved forward still, but slowly. Nevertheless, the miles
were put behind them with an obstinate determination. With
some 300 miles to go to reach the Tunga Bhadra River, and
more to outflank the hordes of Rangapore and join up with
the British advance, the journey was bound to take many
days. The terrain was far from easy, and he had to avoid the
city of Bangalore and its military garrison, the great city
where Lord Cornwallis with a British force had stormed the
fortress in 1791. Rivers had to be forded, and valuable time
and energy lost in finding the fordable places. Ogilvie's
curious clothing grew filthy with dust and sweat, from the
rigours of many hours of riding interspersed with periods
spent on the ground in cover, either for rest or to avoid likely
human contact. The alarm would have gone out widely by
this time and he would be a much wanted man in
Ootacamund.

He had been all kinds of a fool, and this he knew. But it
was too late to turn back now. It was in success alone that his
salvation lay. As so often along the paths of Empire, as so
often in the past story of British military endeavour, the one
thing that counted was success. A man could be the biggest
fool alive and the biggest rogue, and in success all would be
forgiven, while the greatest genius would have his light
forever extinguished by one single spectacular failure.

Ogilvie frowned into the second sunset, a great blood-red
orb sinking in splendour towards the Malabar Coast and the
Arabian Sea: what, in his case, would constitute success? To
ride in and join a British unit after more than 300 miles of

heat and dust, blinding sun and chilly night, near starvation and saddle-sore—all this would constitute a tribute to the hardness of his physical condition and perhaps his single-minded determination, but in all conscience it would add up to little more!

*   *   *

There were men ahead, not for the first time.

Ogilvie, weary from days in the saddle, pulled himself together with a jerk. He had, that morning, ridden through a native village: the villagers had been friendly and made no attempt to hinder the strange-looking sahib: he had a feeling that his odd garb had given them the idea he was a missionary on God's business bent with Bibles in the Gladstone bag rather than the full-dress uniform of a Highland officer. However that might be, they had told him that the rebel levies of the Rajah of Rangapore were upon the banks of the Tunga Bhadra ahead. On leaving the village he had directed his course westerly, the time having come to start his outflanking movement. The word from the villagers was that the Tunga Bhadra and its rebel holders were some fifteen miles distant and that the western perimeter of the Rangapore force stood so far as was known currently at Koppal on the railway line. If he aimed to cross the line between Gadag and Hubli he would have a chance of avoiding them, but, of course, the farther west he went the better the prospect; and he was now heading as best he could towards the town of Dharwar.

The sight of the men ahead sent him quickly from his horse; dismounted, he crept with the animal into the shelter of some trees with thick undergrowth growing to a helpful height about the trunks. This time, however, luck was not on his side: there was a shout, and some of the men started running towards the spot where he had last been seen. About to ride out and chance it, he heard horses' hooves, distant but closing at a gallop, and soon he saw around a dozen riders coming in to draw the covert. With no weapons, he was helpless. When a bearded face, after some crashing through the undergrowth, was thrust almost into his own, he could do no more than stay where he was and make an attempt to smile and gain the man's friendship. There was a shout in a dialect unfamiliar to Ogilvie, though he caught the word sahib. Armed with the old-fashioned, long-barrelled *jezails*, the others closed in, led by a thick, squat rider, heavily bearded, turbaned, and with blackened teeth.

This man stared at Ogilvie for several moments before uttering. Then in a throaty voice he said in English, "A sahib. Who are you, and what is your business?"

"I come in peace, as a friend," Ogilvie answered.

"A friend? Yet you hide from us. Why is this?"

Ogilvie shrugged. "I do not know who you are, therefore I am careful."

"Then," the man said with an oily smile, "how do you know you are a friend, sahib?"

"You're quite right," Ogilvie admitted, and laughed. "I don't know. I only hope. May I take it you don't intend me harm?"

There was no reply at first, but a muttered conference took place, then the leader said, "Come out into the open, sahib. You have weapons?"

"None."

"Nevertheless, move out slowly and with your arms above your head. I warn you of this, that we have weapons."

"So I see." Ogilvie came out from cover, warily. He was given a thorough personal search by one of the men, while another held a *jezail* against his chest, its rusty bayonet pricking the cloth of his suit.

"Your business, sahib?" the leader asked.

Ogilvie shrugged. "A traveller, a salesman."

"A poor one." The Indian's gaze ran over his clothing, critically. "One of little wealth, whose wares are of no use, yes? The horse is thin and hungry, and the British sahibs do not usually treat their horses so, or their dogs, which are better nourished than the Untouchables." He paused, his eyes glittering. "It is unusual to find salesmen hiding in bushes, I think. There is a story that comes to us by word of mouth, from the British garrison in the city of Coimbatore as I understand. Sahib, I believe you to be an officer of the British Raj, and not a salesman."

"Is that so?" Ogilvie responded coolly. "And you? You are a good friend of the Raj?"

The man laughed, catching the eyes of his followers. "There are various sorts of friend, sahib! I am no rebel, and no friend of the Rajah who seeks to wage war against the Raj, but I am not notably devoted to the Raj and the great white Queen who dwells in England." He laughed again. "Only a little devoted!"

"Your devotion is financial, perhaps?"

The native inclined his head. "You are wise, sahib, very wise. Money brings loyalty—"

"And there is a price on the head of this British officer of whom you speak?"

"Not a price, sahib, that is, not a direct promise of reward. But that value would flow from a handing over I am certain."

"I see. And what you're saying is, that if the officer was to pay more than that value, your loyalties would undergo a change?"

"They would undoubtedly stretch, sahib. Most undoubtedly so."

"And if the officer sahib had no money?"

"That would be most unfortunate. But it is possible that in his bags the officer sahib would have much money." The eyes gleamed avariciously; naturally, if the Gladstone bag and the carpet-bag had contained gold, the bandit would have taken it and still claimed his reward by handing his prisoner over to the authorities, shrugging away the disappearance of the gold as having been removed by wicked marauders before the sahib was lucky enough to fall into his rescuing hands. The Indian passed an order to his ruffianly crew and a man came forward and took the two bags from Ogilvie. Opened, the

139

full splendour of kilt, sporran and somewhat crushed feathered bonnet, together with the green doublet of the Royal Strathspey, was wonderfully revealed. The leader, clasping his hands, expressed pleasure as the uniform was brought out. "The missing officer sahib without a doubt, a captain sahib as I see from the beautifulness of the badges, yes! A sahib of the soldiers with the musical instrument that squeals like many pigs."

"I understood that you in India liked the pipes?"

"We like also the pig, Captain sahib."

"You're of the Hindu faith?"

"Yes, Captain sahib." The native peered again into the bags, now empty but for some residue of bread. "There is no money, no gold. No rupees."

"No."

"Then we shall ride for the British garrison at Bangalore, Captain sahib."

"I think," Ogilvie said, feeling the start of sheer desperation, "that some arrangement can be come to—"

"No rupees, no bargaining," the leader said with an air of finality. "I do not trust the promise of the British sahibs since a sergeant sahib from a British regiment refused to meet my charges afterwards for my sister, whose services I had sold to him in Bangalore."

*   *   *

Suffering for the sins of omission of an unknown British sergeant, Ogilvie rode eastwards under a strong guard, his bags repacked and balanced behind the weary neck of his horse. The leader of the group engaged him in conversation, assiduously trying to establish his importance to the Raj and the British Army, the better and more fruitfully to conduct his negotiations with the officer sahib commanding at Bangalore. Although nothing was said to this effect in so many words, Ogilvie was well aware that he would not be produced physically until a price had been agreed; there would be a period, long or short, of incarceration where the British would not look. It was a disagreeable prospect to say the least; and a forlorn end to all his hopes of getting into the action to the north. The future was now implacably bleak and he would have dealt his own case the most mortal of blows. Sir Clarence's fury would be boundless, and there would be even more disgrace. For a British officer from a famous regiment to end up as an item in a native bandit's box of bargain-basement tricks would be a considerable embarrassment to the Raj . . .

*　　*　　*

In far distant Calcutta, the seat of governance of the Raj, matters were inexorably in train by now. The telegraph had been busy between Ootacamund, Madras, Secunderabad and the capital—and with Peshawar, Nowshera and Murree also; and later in the office of the Military Secretary to the Earl of Elgin, Viceroy of India, Lieutenant-General Sir Iain Ogilvie was left to kick his heels, a process the Northern Army Commander was unaccustomed to, while Colonel Durand, the Military Secretary, conferred urgently with His Excellency. Sir Iain was kept waiting for half an hour before Durand returned.

"H.E. will see you, sir, but I advise caution. The mood's bleak." Durand, a tall man, as straight-backed as Sir Iain, pulled at his moustache. "I dessay you can imagine . . . everyone's at him. India Office, Foreign Office, Downing Street, the Palace. Berlin and Stockholm. Ambassadors galore." He paused, looking gravely at the Northern Army Commander—who, in disregard of the Dress Regulations for the Army, still, as a General, wore the kilt of the Royal Strathspey. "I've explained that your interview's been sought on a personal matter, Sir Iain—"

"Quite right, since it is." Sir Iain spoke brusquely, not in

141

the least relishing what lay ahead of him: he was not a seeker of favours. "Lead on, Durand, don't let us waste time, mine or HE's."

Durand nodded and turned away. Sir Iain, kilt swinging round sun-browned knees beneath the scarlet tunic of the General Staff, followed the Military Secretary along a corridor and up to the great Marble Hall of Government House and thence to the private office of the Viceroy, a large room containing, as in Farrar-Drumm's headquarters, portraits of men whose names rang down the years of Empire, a room dominated, as in all Britain's overseas dominions and colonies, by Her Majesty Queen Victoria, Empress of India, mother of all her peoples, Defender of the Faith, a small dog crouched obsequiously at her feet as she stared sternly from a window in Windsor Castle. Lord Elgin sat, as though in conscious symbolism, immediately below his monarch; and Sir Iain, having the uncomfortable feeling that Her Majesty was turning disdainfully aside from him as he approached the Viceroy on a personal mission for a miscreant, was put off his stroke; but only for the brief moment of silence before His Excellency uttered.

"Well, Ogilvie?"

The tone was tart; Sir Iain at once resented it and felt his caution vanish. "Not well for my son, Your Excellency."

"Quite." Lord Elgin smiled; there was sympathy in him. "Sit down, Ogilvie." He indicated a gilded chair, and Sir Iain thanked him perfunctorily and sat. "An unpleasant business, and I'm sorry, genuinely sorry."

"It can be ameliorated, sir."

"How?"

"Forget the royal involvement."

Elgin made a deprecatory gesture. "With pleasure—if I could! But that's the whole point at issue—"

"Stuff-and-nonsense!"

"Your tone won't help you, Ogilvie."

Sir Iain simmered. "I apologise, sir. The phrase was rude. I withdraw it. What I mean is this: the crime, if crime there

142

is, is military. The person, or personage, involved is immaterial. Or damn well should be! A soldier should be judged by his actions, not by his companions."

Elgin lifted an eyebrow. "His responsibilities, I think, General?"

"All right. I admit the point. But a life's a life, no more. Had it been a common soldier, there wouldn't have been all this fuss, sir! That's what I wish to state. And something else."

"Well?"

"My son's no coward, sir. No coward at all. His record speaks for that."

"I'd most certainly not suppose, *prima facie,* anyone with the name of Ogilvie to be a coward," the Viceroy said diplomatically, "and of course his record's already been brought to my attention. A very good young officer, I agree, and I'm very sorry as I've said. However, my hands are tied and I fail to see what you expect me to do?"

"I repeat, sir, have the case treated on its merits and leave out the overtones of royalty, which are enough to sway any Court Martial. I know—I've sat on 'em before now!" Sir Iain leaned forward heavily, pugnaciously, almost as though about to wave a broadsword in the Viceroy's face. "Surely it's within your Viceregal prerogative to tell the damn Judge Advocate-General not to prosecute on a basis of the royal personage involved?"

The Viceroy shrugged. "Perhaps, but my answer's no, Ogilvie, whatever my prerogative. I remind you of this: rank counts in *all* spheres." Elgin spoke with reproof. "Had you not been of the rank you are, holding the appointment you hold, do you imagine for one moment I would have consented to see you on such a matter, which is not only *ultra vires* from my standpoint, but also *sub judice?*"

"I have little Latin!" Sir Iain snapped.

Elgin seemed about to utter an angry retort, but did not do so. Instead he said mildly, "You'd do better to be reticent, my dear fellow. You should not try to force me to discuss the case further—in its very nature it's bound to come before my office at a later stage and that is when I shall consider it, not before. You should not do your son a disservice by such insistence now." Elgin paused. "It's not like you to seek special treatment, Ogilvie. Women, of course, are different . . . I appreciate a mother's feelings, but—"

"I have *not* been urged by my wife, sir!"

Elgin smiled gently. "I would be most astonished if you had not. It's very natural, you know. But allow me to say this: as General Officer Commanding the Northern Army at Murree you have the complete confidence of both the Commander-in-Chief and myself, also of Her Majesty. But command of an army also involves command of a wife . . . I hope you'll not think me impertinent, though I fear you do judging from the look upon your face. Let us consider something more profitable to all of us, Ogilvie: the present whereabouts of your son, which is causing us anxiety as well as you. With your knowledge of him, you may be able to help . . ."

Sir Iain held his temper in check and the conversation continued a little longer; Ogilvie senior was unable to offer any suggestion beyond the fact that he was convinced James would turn up in honourable circumstances provided he did not fall, or had not already fallen, a prey to bandits or the practitioners of *thuggee*. When dismissed from the Viceregal presence he was met in the ante-room by the Military Secretary.

"Well, sir?"

"Well my arse, Durand! Damn feller had the bloody cheek to suggest I was wife-ridden, henpecked—can you imagine!" Sir Iain raised his fist, turned, and brandished it at Lord Elgin's closed door: a *havildar* of the Viceregal Bodyguard, all scarlet and gold, looked shocked at the extravagances of sahibs. "I tell you who's at the root of all this, Durand: that old woman Farrar-Drumm, about as much use to the army as a fart in a frying-pan!" He proceeded down the corridor towards the Marble Hall, seething. "Be so good as to call my carriage, Durand." And he added bitterly, "Henpecked indeed!"

Behind him, the Military Secretary smiled an enigmatic smile.

Twelve

AN IMPRECATION CAME, very suddenly, from the leader of
Ogilvie's bandit escort. He held up his hand, reined in his
own horse, and halted his men, speaking rapidly in the local
dialect. The men dismounted; in English the leader said,
"Take cover, sahib."

"What's up now?"

"There are men ahead, beyond the rising ground—"

"I saw nothing."

"Do not argue, sahib, but take cover, and do not try to
escape." He pointed. "Over there, in the trees. As far back
as you can go, so that the horses are not seen."

With two *jezails* covering him, Ogilvie obeyed the order.
The group sank into the trees, moving fast, and when far
enough they halted and remained still as death, holding their
horses and murmuring low words of comfort to keep the
animals quiet. Ogilvie pondered the development: if the
newcomers were British troops, he would be no better and
no worse off, though it could be assumed that his present
captor would have no welcome for them; he had his
negotiations to conduct, and would not want his prize
snatched from him. Ogilvie watched the natives closely,
scanned the bearded faces, the capable brown fingers curled
around the triggers of the *jezails*. If there was a British
presence, then he might, just might, be able to make a run
for it in the heat of the coming fight. On the other hand,
Ogilvie was becoming increasingly aware of the appalling
stupidity, as he saw it now, of his action in as it were
releasing himself from arrest; to rejoin by way of the nearest
British unit had been his initial intention, and that was

perhaps what he should now try to do. He found himself unable to come to a decision; weary and hungry, he procrastinated, telling himself that events might be left to follow their own course, though it was obvious enough that a British patrol, finding him in his strange company, would take him back to base for interrogation—and in any case, since they would obviously be in communication with Bangalore, they would already have the word that he was to be picked up.

Now there were sounds from the distance, though so far nothing could be seen. The sounds indicated a number of horsemen: there was a jingling of harness. A little later there was song—native song. They were not, therefore, troops of the British Army. Still the bandits remained immobile and silent; the leader turned towards Ogilvie and spoke into his ear: "Not a sound, sahib, or you will suffer." The bayonet of one of the *jezails* pricked Ogilvie's spine unpleasantly. Moments passed; the riders came nearer. In the worst possible of all places for the hidden group, the newcomers halted and dismounted at the fringe of the trees. Ogilvie could see them through the trunks, spasmodically; he saw uniforms, gaudy ones and dishevelled. Definitely not a British unit . . . after a moment a man—two men, then a third—moved into the trees and flung themselves on the ground, almost as though seeking cover themselves. Ogilvie tensed, something of the true facts permeating. He had no time to consider further before the presence of his group was given away: a horse neighed, loudly. There was an oath from the leader, who swung his *jezail* as if to slaughter the animal, but thought better of it. His face murderous, he struck the horse's holder with the butt of his weapon and gave orders for his band to move away fast and to mount as soon as they were clear of the trees.

"A close eye upon the officer sahib—and a *jezail*." He turned to look back as his men moved out; already the pursuit had started, the uniformed natives crashing through the undergrowth and discharging rifles. Bullets zoomed and

147

sang, ricocheting from the tree-trunks, whining close to the departing bandits. Ogilvie suffered a close shave as lead cut across his shoulder, stinging and drawing blood. One of the bandits gave a loud yell and pitched forward to roll in agony on the ground: the rest hurried on, leaving him to die. Rusty steel penetrated Ogilvie's back. Once clear of the trees the bandits mounted and rode like the wind, forming an escort around Ogilvie. Shots followed them, and another man crashed from his horse to lie still, with blood pouring from his head. Behind them the pursuers rushed out from the trees, yelling, firing rapidly and with good effect. The bandit leader was hit and fell, then two more men went down and a bullet took Ogilvie's horse. As the animal crumpled, Ogilvie was pitched head first, the Gladstone bag and carpet bag thudding down close by. No notice was taken of him now; the survivors fled on with the uniformed riders pounding after them. Alongside Ogilvie as he sat up, a horse was pulled to its haunches, hooves flailing, only just missing him as its feet came down to earth. Its rider looked down, eyebrows lifted.

"A white sahib! You keep strange company, sahib. Who are you?"

Ogilvie got to his feet and dusted down his suit. He answered coolly, "One who was attacked and was being carried off. I am grateful for your interference! May I ask who you are?"

The horseman laughed. "You may, and I shall answer. I am an officer of the army of His Highness the Rajah of Rangapore." He studied Ogilvie critically. "You appear surprised, my friend, and upset also. Why is this?"

It was in fact not surprise that Ogilvie had registered; he had approached the truth earlier, but the confirmation and its implications were far from pleasing. He said off-handedly, "I'm not upset, why should I be? If you'll be so kind as to put me on the track for Bangalore, I shall be grateful, friend. Also, perhaps, a horse?"

Again the man laughed. He had a warrior's face, and a

distinguished one, not unpleasant when he smiled. "A horse most certainly. But not the track for Bangalore. The track north for the Kistna River, sahib. You will come with us. If you have been long in this part, you will know that His Highness is on the march—and no sahib can be left behind once caught!"

*   *   *

Masefield's brigade began to close the north bank of the Kistna; the order came down the column to halt for a night's bivouac with the Kistna now only some fifteen miles ahead. On their flanks, but distantly, the other formations had also moved down to confront the rebel forces in support of the Nizam. Lord Brora, returning from a conference held by the Brigadier-General after the halt had been ordered, was confident and anxious to engage.

"Our hand is strong," he told his assembled officers. "We ourselves have an excellent brigade and will be ably supported by the cavalry and the guns, together with more infantry." He indicated two positions on the map that had been set up on a blackboard in the light of a guard lantern. "There's the Kistna, we are there. You see, gentlemen? There—and there—and there are the other columns. We march at first light for the Kistna, and the expectation is that we shall be in action shortly afterwards. The rebel forces are expected to advance along a broad front, and we shall be there to meet them. And to stop them."

Black asked, "Do you think the Rajah will make a frontal attack, then, sir?"

Brora laughed contemptuously. "He'll not attack at all, he'll *be* attacked!"

"You mean he won't have word that we're marching to meet him?"

"It's doubtful, Captain Black. The damn natives are in no position to employ intelligence services, are they?"

"They have the bush telegraph, sir."

"Oh, I know all about the bush telegraph and its so-called miracles, Captain Black, and I am in no way worried."

"And the Brigadier-General?"

"He spoke of it, and advised that we all be on our guard for surprises, certainly. That was no more than a prudent warning. I repeat, it will be *we* who move to the attack, putting the Rajah's levies on the defensive from the start. It will be part of our orders to prevent any of the Rajah's army slipping through between us and the columns to east and west of us, but if they should slip through, then they will be mopped up by two reserve brigades presently marching south from Secunderabad." Brora drew himself up. "Now I have my own orders for the battalion, and you will take note, Captain Black."

"Yes, sir."

"No one is to slip through. No one is to slip past me. I will not be outflanked." His voice had risen. "There are to be the usual scouts sent out ahead, but this time more so. A half-company will extend to the left of my advance, and a half-company to the right. *My* advance will be very broad indeed. Is that understood, Captain Black?"

Black nodded. "It is, sir, it is."

"Then see to it. And see that every man knows that his duty is to Her Majesty, to the Nizam, and to me. The routes north from the Kistna are to be held to the death—to the death, d'you hear me?"

The Scots officers signified that they had heard, and were then dismissed. Robin Stuart walked away thoughtfully with Bruce Fraser, now acting in command of Ogilvie's company. "I hope Brora won't throw the regiment away," he remarked wryly. "They're a damn fine bunch, the best when all's said and done." He sighed. "I wish to God Dornoch was back with us tomorrow!"

"And James."

"Amen to that! Not," Stuart added quickly, "that you'll not do as well in his place, Bruce." He hesitated. "It's just that he's been in all the fights since we first came out to

India—he's an essential part of the regiment and in effect he's been driven from it by Brora. I've a feeling it'll bring us poor luck not to have him. If we could just get some word of him . . ."

"The only word'll be of his re-arrest, worse luck—or that he's fallen to bandits."

"Well, you never know. He may pull something out of the bag."

"Such as what?" Fraser sounded sceptical. "And come to that—what bag?"

The question could have been considered rhetorical; Stuart, who had no ready answer, let it go as such. The two officers went to their supper, served up by the field kitchens. When supper was over and the men in their bivouacs, sleep was hard to come by. Even seasoned campaigners had their nagging doubts before action, and the forthcoming action promised to be on a far bigger scale than Frontier patrol activity and probes against the Pathans of the North. And Lord Dornoch was going to be much missed; he was their trusted leader, their Colonel, and all the men would follow him without question. Brora was not the man to inspire them to anything but dislike—and fear. Fear had its place in the scheme of things and was a useful adjunct to discipline; but of itself it was far from enough. The Regimental Sergeant-Major, as he walked the column under night's cloak, found all his worries as expressed earlier to James Ogilvie returning in full measure. The men were restless, and he knew well why. Not that there would be no keenness to win, to uphold the name of the regiment—the Scots would never hold back in a fight. If they didn't have the opportunity to fight in the field, they would fight in the streets of Glasgow . . . his worries were not to do with that! But somehow the fire would be missing . . . Cunningham tried hard to shrug off his black and doleful mood. He strode on through the darkness, past those who could find no sleep and who were occupying themselves in giving their rifles an extra pull-through with strips of two-by-four, so as to ensure impeccable cleanliness

151

of the barrels when the bullets began to fly next day. He visited the outlying picquets at their posts, having a brief word with each man, noting gladly that a full alertness was being maintained and finding fault with only one man.

"Lance-Corporal Wicks, your kilt's awry."

"Sir!" Wicks rectified his dress, and was re-inspected by the Regimental Sergeant-Major.

"Aye, that'll do. We'll not face the enemy improperly dressed, Wicks, and you as a lance should set an example."

"Aye, sir."

"Then watch yourself." Cunningham moved on, making back towards the bivouacs. Lance-Corporal Wicks would suck his teeth for a while and would pass it on that the old bugger thought he was back on parade in Peshawar or Invermore; which was part of the intention. Routine and detail took a soldier's mind off death, and for an RSM to behave as usual was all a part of routine and had its steadying effect in action. The day would be indeed lost when a Warrant Officer's eagle eye dimmed. Cunningham smiled to himself, feeling a trifle better. Never mind the Colonel, the regiment was still sound in basis and would give a good account of itself when the rebels engaged. He went to his bivouac and turned in, lay awake for a while, then slept.

In the early dawn the bugles sounded loud and clear for Reveille and men began to stir, being shouted from their sleep by the busy sergeants and corporals and turning out to wash and shave. Rising, Cunningham saw Lord Brora already walking briskly up and down in the morning cool, turning as smartly as a sentry each time he reached the limit of his self-set beat, the early sun striking fire from his buttons and badges of rank and from the shining, polished leather of his Sam Browne belt. He was, Cunningham thought almost grudgingly, a fine physical specimen, every inch a Colonel. A pity he had not the mental attributes to match the physique. A degree of compassion would not have come amiss . . . a touch, not obtrusive, but held ready for use, as it were, when required, was part of the make-up of command in

152

Cunningham's opinion. The Adjutant was without it, to be sure, but Lord Dornoch had it and so had young Ogilvie . . .

Lord Brora halted in his up-and-down march and saw the RSM. "Good morning, Mr Cunningham."

"Good morning, sir." Hastily seizing his Wolseley helmet and setting it upon his head. Cunningham saluted.

"A moment, if you please."

"Sir!" Cunningham marched forward, halted in front of the Colonel, and once again saluted.

"I saw you prowling about last night, Sar'nt-Major. Is that a good thing?"

"In my view, sir, it is."

"I see. What's the purpose, may I ask?"

"To keep an eye open that all's correct, sir."

"You don't trust the NCOs—the sergeant of the guard—the Captain of the Day either, perhaps?"

"I do, sir, of course—"

"Ah, but there's no 'of course', Sar'nt-Major. NCOs can nod, so can officers, though only once with me. However, you say you trust them. Should you not therefore be *seen* to do so, by not perambulating the lines like an old woman who fears burglars beneath her bed?"

Cunningham's mouth opened in sheer astonishment and indignation. He was shaken to the core. Never in all his years of service had he been likened, by any person from Field-Marshal to private soldier, to an old woman fearful of her bedtime security. He was speechless. Brora said, "I think you are shocked, Sar'nt-Major."

"Aye, sir. I am."

"Not a bad thing," Brora said brutally. "You are too complacent—the whole damn battalion needs a shock if you ask me. They may get it today! There's one thing more: Captain Ogilvie."

"Sir?"

"Erase him from your mind. I'm far from blind, Mr Cunningham. I am a person of some sensibility. You have been over friendly with Captain Ogilvie. Warrant officers

153

have not the Queen's commission—I shall not make too much of that, because I think you see yourself simply in a fatherly light. He and you have served together for a long time—I appreciate all that. But for your own good, forget him now. He will not be rejoining the battalion whether he is alive or not."

Cunningham found speech. "Then it will be a sad day for the battalion, sir. Captain Ogilvie is a fine officer, the best there is—and he's no coward!"

"That's for the Court Martial to say, not you. Have a care, Mr Cunningham, and do not be led into impertinence and even insolence—"

"Sir, I am the Regimental Sergeant-Major, not a freshly made-up lance-corporal still wet behind the ears, sir! I resent what you say, sir. I resent it very strongly indeed. I have always done my duty, and done my best for the regiment. If Lord Dornoch were here—"

"Lord Dornoch, always Lord Dornoch! Well, he's not here but I am. You would do well to remember that everything Lord Dornoch did was wrong. Wrong, wrong, wrong!" Brora, his eyes flashing fire, underlined each repetition of the word with a crash of his riding-boot on the hard earth of the Indian plain. "Remember this as well, at your peril: I have not the power to break you to the ranks, Mr Cunningham, but by God I have the power to order your Court Martial, and I have the power to place you in arrest meanwhile and suspend you from your duties! What have you to say to that?"

Cunningham's chest went out and his shoulders stiffened. "With respect, sir, I have this to say: you will have a need of me today if the men are to fight well. If, God forbid, the day should go against us, you would have much explaining to do, sir, to the GOC, for sending your battalion into action with your Regimental Sergeant-Major in arrest, sir! I take it that will be all, sir."

Cunningham gave a swinging salute and executed a crashing about-turn. He marched away, left-right-left with

154

his back straight and his shoulders square. Christ, he thought to himself, the man's verging on madness, a major acting in the rank of colonel in command of a fighting Scots battalion to be stamping his foot like a bairn—and worse, to have committed the cardinal crime of running down a CO to a Warrant Officer. It was a disgrace, nothing short of that, and God help the men this day.

*   *   *

The brigade moved out behind the pipes and drums as soon as breakfast had been taken, Lord Brora riding in the lead of the Royal Strathspey as though nothing had been said, swaggering along the track and talking loudly to the Adjutant of what he intended to inflict upon the "damned heathen" the moment his scouts raised the rebel van. Cunningham, marching up and down the Scots line, keeping an eye on the NCOs, wondered at the Colonel's gall. The man seemed most extraordinarily resilient, that was sure. He had, in fact, spoken with impeccable politeness to Cunningham as the battalion had fallen in for the march, which seemed to indicate a powerful ability to assume that others forgot as quickly as he did. Cunningham shook his head in perplexity; Brora was an enigma to him—an enigma to his officers as well, he suspected. He wasn't strictly mad, he wasn't even entirely irrational normally; but he took some getting used to! The march continued throughout the morning with no more than a fifteen-minute halt to rest the men and horses and replenish the water-bottles from a stream. By order from Brigade the pace was being forced, and the men were ready enough for even a short break. Cunningham, despite the Colonel's strictures earlier, walked down the resting line, having a word with the sergeants and corporals as he went. He remembered his reflections of the night before: that the battalion was sound in basis. This morning he was back to gloom again. The men had a dour look, and they seemed morose. There was more grousing than there should have been, and Cunningham began to sense, alarmingly, an actual lack of stomach for the fight, something worse than he had so far feared. Even the NCOs spoke grudgingly, as though there was something at the backs of their minds, some fear that orders might not always be implicitly obeyed. Cunningham was convinced that the men themselves were sound yet; the general lack of spirit was due, he was quite sure, to the Colonel personally. It was a feeling that he might prove lacking in battle, perhaps—not as to his courage, but as to his tactics. Officers who were over-impulsive could be a danger to their men, liable to do stupid things. Cunningham's belief grew that the battalion had no confidence in its command; though broadly it would be the Brigadier-General who would decide the course of the action and how the battalions were to be deployed, much would depend upon the individual colonels. Cunningham brooded uneasily as the bugles sounded the fall-in once again. Lord Brora swung himself into the saddle and lifted his hand and the pipes and drums struck up and the sergeants began to shout the step, and down and down again came the marching boots to stir up the dry dust. The vultures gathered; they had been there all along—they were inseparable from any Indian march—but now, suddenly as they came closer to the Kistna River, they were there in force, wheeling in the sky, swooping down, uttering their harsh cries, lifting again on their immense black wing spans, beaks eager, scrawny necks poised, ever watchful for the dead. Greedy bastards, Cunningham thought, aren't they ever satisfied?

*   *   *

A mounted subaltern was seen coming back from ahead, riding hell-for-leather from the advanced scouting party. He pulled up his sweat-lathered horse beside the Brigadier-General, whose khaki-drill jacket had a covering of fine dust.

"Sir, a body of men ahead—"

"Enemy?"

"No, sir. From an Indian cavalry regiment—and all dead, sir."

Masefield stared. "All dead?"

"I'm afraid so, sir. The horses too. Throats cut in every case, ear to ear, sir." The subaltern's face was white beneath its dust. "It was a horrible sight."

Masefield nodded sombrely. "I've no doubt it was. How far ahead?"

"Two miles, sir."

"No warning, no sound of attack?"

"None, sir. I believe they'd been dead for some hours, perhaps longer. The blood was dried out, and the vultures were there, of course." The young officer paused. 'Frankly, sir, there's not much left."

Masefield nodded once again and said crisply, "Very well. Return to your scouts." He caught the eye of his Brigade Major. "Messages to the battalion commanders, if you please, Major, giving them the report. And pass the word that we must expect attack at any time."

A runner was despatched down the column. Masefield rode on, studying the land ahead through field glasses. There was a feeling of much tension now, tension that spread right through the brigade as the word reached the battalions. Lord Brora showed excitement and impatience and began to harry his Adjutant. Black, scowling, passed the harassment on to the company commanders, and via the colour-sergeants it reached the rank and file, where it stopped and festered. In due course each man in the marching column came past the remains of the Indian Army cavalry unit. The badges and guidons proclaimed a squadron of Skinner's Horse. With action probably imminent, the Brigadier-General decided there was no time for burial parties to operate. The column divided about the bodies and marched on beneath the hoarse indignation of the vultures, which had been disturbed in their meal to rise like a great black cloud as the van of the brigade had approached. As the rearguard passed by, they came

157

down again in a black, funereal flutter. In the meantime no attack had come, and there was no sign of any living persons in the vicinity. The field glasses of the officers could find no indication of any rebel force. They seemed, oddly, to be advancing through and into a vacuum. Soon the broad swathe cut through the land by the Kistna River was reached by the advanced scouts, and once again a rider came back to report, and his report was transmitted by runner to the colonels: still no sign of the enemy. The Kistna, at any rate in the vicinity immediately ahead, was peaceful; and the few natives who had been encountered had had no knowledge of rebel movements.

"I'll be bound!" Brora said sarcastically. "Of course they'll deny any knowledge—until they're put under strong pressure! The buggers have a care for their own hides, and that works both ways. But Masefield can be relied upon to know that, presumably."

They carried on. Within the next hour the whole brigade was upon the banks of the river, the halt had been sounded, and the men fallen out to kick their heels. There was a lot of swearing; such anti-climax was bewildering, and not entirely welcome to men who had been keyed-up for action. The Colonel was acidly furious. "There's been a balls-up," he announced loudly. "Someone's slipped. Well, we all know it's not me, I think!" He turned as a runner came up and saluted him. "Yes?"

"The Brigadier-General's compliments, sir, and all commanding officers are requested to attend Brigade, sir."

"Very well." Lord Brora nodded a dismissal and turned to the Adjutant. "I have a feeling Masefield will want to make camp and remain to await orders from Secunderabad. I, on the other hand, have other ideas. You will rest the men and horses, Captain Black, but allow no sinking back into sloth."

Brora mounted his horse and went at a canter towards Brigade, leaving many questions in the still air behind him.

Thirteen

THE RAJAH'S MEN had turned for the west initially; after a long ride in that direction they altered for the north and crossed the Tunga Bhadra by a ford, with the waters swirling along the horses' bellies and Ogilvie under close guard as he had been throughout. Before leaving the scene of the slaughter of the bandits, they had opened Ogilvie's bags and had been mightily surprised at what they had found therein.

"An officer sahib, no less! An officer of the Raj! His Highness will be most pleased. Tell me, sahib; do you come to spy, perhaps?"

"No. To rejoin my regiment."

"And your regiment's whereabouts, sahib?"

"In Bangalore," Ogilvie had answered smoothly, "which is where I asked to go."

The rebel officer shrugged. "We shall see. The Rajah will bring out all the facts. Now to horse." He gave an order to his men, a mount was brought for Ogilvie, and the long ride started. They went back, in the early stages, along much the same track as Ogilvie had traversed with the bandits; but went far beyond the point where he had been picked up. They passed thereafter through country as arid as that had gone before, until they neared the river and the irrigation that brought some green and cultivation to relieve the drear, dusty monotony. Once across the Tunga Bhadra the ride was again northerly; throughout the course of it there was little conversation, just a silent concentration on getting where they were going. Ogilvie hoped that they might fall in with a British patrol extended from the army

159

marching down from Secunderabad, which surely by now must be not far off the Kistna. He was unable to pick up any clues that might help him to some assessment of the British position, though there was an urgency about the riders, as if to get him to Rangapore was vital, and that might possibly indicate a known proximity of forces sent to succour the Nizam of Hyderabad.

It was towards nightfall when the party raised the towers of the old city of Rangapore. It was a picturesque sight as the sun went down in brilliant colours. Rangapore was built at the foot of rising ground, and much of the city climbed the slope of the hill with narrow alleys running between small dwellings, built in more recent centuries outside the ancient fortifying walls, high and enclosing, within which was situated the Rajah's palace, acting as the central bastion of what in effect was a fortress. Ogilvie rode towards high iron gates, the party making its way past a stinking open drain that carried all waste, human and vegetable and animal, out of Rangapore. Crowds jostled them as they pushed through, and there was some exchange of badinage from which the Rajah's officer held himself aloof, gazing ahead haughtily. They halted at the entry and the gates were opened to admit them. They rode on behind the high wall into a central courtyard, a cool place it would be, Ogilvie thought, even in the heat of day: there were shady trees, and fountains playing despite central India's perennial shortage of water— even in winter, for the winters were dry enough—and tinny music came from an open window to the left. There was, curiously for a fortress housing a warlike man and a rebel, a pervading sense of peace and tranquillity.

Ogilivie was ordered to dismount. Under guard, he was taken into the palace, through an immense hall, up a gracefully curving flight of marble stairs, along a corridor and into a high-set room with a single window that looked over the wall and across the city. His bags were left with him and he was told to dress himself in his uniform. Then he was left alone; as a natural act, after the escort had gone, he tried the door. Equally naturally, it was locked; and would be guarded as well.

Ogilvie went across to the window and leaned out: it was obvious enough why no bars had been considered necessary for his confinement. The drop was long, the ground hard, and the wall sheer, with no apparent handholds or footholds. To try to get down that way would be suicide. Forward planning would have to wait yet!

*   *   *

Many a maharajah and rajah of the princely states of India had been given an English education: Eton or Harrow followed by Oxford or Cambridge. Sometimes even the Royal Military College at Sandhurst, or the Academy at Woolwich if their interests lay in the guns of the Royal Regiment of Artillery. Many indeed—but not the Rajah of Rangapore. His smell assailed the nostrils from far off; his clothing was filthy, as though never changed from one year's end to another. His Highness would have been much cleaned up by Eton, and he would in his current state have given apoplexy to the company serjeant-majors at the RMC. But he did speak English of a sort, haltingly, clumsily and grinning from a nut-cracker face as Ogilvie advanced to meet him in the full-dress uniform of the Royal Strathspey, an armed soldier at each side.

"British soldier?"

"Yes, Your Highness."

"Vairy fine. Come." The Rajah beckoned and Ogilvie moved nearer. The Rajah, who seemed to be in his middle thirties or thereabouts, was seated on a throne far more resplendent than any sat in by Her Majesty Queen Victoria: for a start, it was of solid gold. Or so Ogilvie assumed, since brass would scarcely have been a fitting setting for the rubies and emeralds and diamonds that glowed richly from the arms and legs of it, and from the Rajah's sky-blue turban. The feather that rose from the turban was set into a clasp bearing

161

a diamond the size of a half-crown. As Ogilvie came within range, the Rajah leaned forward, his eyes curious. He touched the doublet, the kilt, the sporran, the *skean dhu* in the stocking. He gabbled to himself. Ogilvie stood at attention, holding his Highland bonnet beneath his left arm—until it was taken from him by a powerful grab and held in the Rajah's arms, caressingly, as though it were some pet lap-dog. The Rajah gabbled on, then spoke his appalling English.

"Raj is good. Queen-Empress good also."

"Yes, Your Highness."

"Nizam not good." An arm was raised and swished through the air as though it held a sabre to strike the luckless Nizam dead. "Nizam, I spit on."

He did; the gob flew past Ogilvie and landed on priceless marble inlaid with gold. "I am friend to great Raj, and great Queen-Empress." He added, "No fear!"

Ogilvie raised his eyebrows, wondering if the Rajah had somehow picked up an English schoolboy expression and was making opposite use of it, or whether he was reassuring his prisoner that he intended no harm to him. Before elucidation could come, His Highness proceeded. "Nizam of Hyderabad is wicked person. I send my army. I will kill him. I am strong, you know 'ow strong?"

"No, Your Highness."

"A hundred thousand men strong."

Ogilvie stared: he had had no idea a provincial rajah could command support of that order. In India, one learned every day—unless, of course, the Rajah's arithmetic was at fault, which was possible. "A lot of men, Your Highness."

"Much lot, yes. Also arsenals. Guns, bullets. Little guns, big guns, *great* guns led by elephants. I have seven thousand elephants with armour." Suddenly the Rajah laughed; it was more of a giggle in point of fact. "Ears go flap, flap." He lifted his hands to the side of his turban, and performed a double flapping movement, his eyes, coal-black and small, looking merry.

"Seven thousand flap, flap," Ogilvie said sardonically, wondering at the childlike action.

"Not. Fourteen thousand flap, flap."

Ogilvie took a chance: it couldn't do much harm if it went wrong. He lifted his own hands and put them to his ears. Solemnly, in his splendid regimentals, he wagged. "Flap, flap," he said. The Rajah's merriment increased; he laughed, he roared, he flapped, tears ran down his cheeks. He was beside himself. He rose from his throne and embraced Ogilvie.

"Raj officer sahib good like Raj, like Queen-Empress. Vairy good sahib. I like. You like?"

"Yes, Your Highness." As politely as possible Ogilvie eased himself from the embrace. There was gold and silk and precious mineral upon the Rajah's raiment, but there was stale food also. "I like."

A giggle. "Flap, flap?" The eyes twinkled.

"Flap, flap." They were off again.

* * *

Seven thousand was a lot of gun-elephants, a hundred thousand was enough men to disturb the very foundations of the British Raj, let alone the threatened Nizam of Hyderabad. Of course, very many of them, both men and guns to say nothing of the elephants, would be useless in a pitched battle and plenty, in fact, would turn and run at the first fire. Of that hundred thousand a fair proportion would be old, senile even, yet heads to count in the Rajah's boastful roll. Many would be sick — yet it still left a very large army to put into the field, many of whom would be brave enough. It was Ogilvie's plain duty, now that he was in Rangapore, to find out all the facts. Actual effective strength, disposition of units, direction of advance, aims and intentions, the whole overall strategy and the tactics to be used. Unfortunately the Rajah had similar desires and was able to formulate them

163

through the agency of a high officer whom he introduced as his General. The General, whose name was Rajeshwar Acharya, was a tall man, very military, every inch a soldier, and with excellent English. He had obvious authority in the Rajah's court and seemed well able to supply the military expertise: through General Rajeshwar Acharya, the Rajah at once became a more ominous figure.

"Your English is good, General sahib," Ogilvie remarked politely: he had been bidden to dine with the Rajah and was now seated cross-legged upon a silken cushion of royal blue in front of low tables groaning with filled dishes that His Highness was doing his best to empty.

"Oh, it's good enough," the General said, with an off-hand gesture.

"Learned where, may I ask?"

"The Raj, Captain sahib. I was the *Risaldar*-Major of the Bengal Lancers."

Another shock! "I see," Ogilvie said. *Risaldar*-Major was the highest a Viceroy's Commissioned Officer could attain in the Indian Army, and such a rank was given only to the most loyal and trusted officers. "You surprise me, General sahib. Do you not think your loyalties should be even now to the Raj?"

"No." Rajeshwar Acharya shook his head firmly, his piercing eyes, as black as his master's, holding Ogilvie's. "I was dismissed by sentence of a Court Martial. I refused my Colonel's order to open fire upon men of my own race—more, of my own village."

Ogilvie felt drained inside; his own troubles smote at him like a club. "Truly?" he asked, shaken by the close coincidence.

"Yes, truly indeed. Why do you ask that, Captain sahib? These things have happened before, and will happen again."

"Yes, of course—I had no special reason. I understand your refusal, General sahib. Your Colonel's order was . . . unwise."

"Yet upheld by the Court Martial. The Raj cannot be

164

disobeyed. But it can be fought, Captain sahib, and will be fought. My love for it has been destroyed by injustice."

"And His Highness the Nizam?"

Rajeshwar Acharya gave a harsh laugh. "The Nizam is for the Raj. It supports him, he supports it. The Raj and the Nizam are one and the same, and must be destroyed."

"Both?"

"Yes. The Nizam first, then the Raj. In the Nizam's defeat, great numbers of his men will join the standard of Rangapore."

"But why? What's the purpose? Pique?"

"No. Oh, partly yes, but only partly." The General's gaze swept the guzzling Rajah who, deep in a dish of *pilau*— rice, chicken and sultanas garnished unbelievably with wafer-thin strips of real silver—was quite lost by the conversation in English. "Rangapore is advancing under my direction. It's people have aspirations that must be satisfied, and have little land to call their own. The Nizam is despotic, and we are wearied of rule from Hyderabad. We have risen and shall conquer, and the Raj must beware. Hitherto subject peoples are on the march."

"I see." Ogilvie nibbled at some fruit. "And your first objective, General sahib?"

"To march upon, and take, the city of Hyderabad."

"And the Nizam?"

There was a shrug of indifference. "If he makes good his escape, then so be it. We intend to depose him and make him a powerless figure of ridicule, one who will never take up power again, but we do not plan his death necessarily."

"You wish to replace him by your own Rajah?" Ogilvie looked across at His Highness, who was being attended by a serving girl offering yet more food: the Rajah's face showed the clear evidence of greed, and there was more upon his clothing. He seemed an unlikely person to rule a great state such as Hyderabad.

The General answered Ogilvie's question. "If events run thus, so be it. It would be good. But that is not necessarily

165

my intention. My aim is rather to free Rangapore from subjection and domination. If a Nizam can succeed who will keep his hands off Rangapore, then both I and His Highness will be satisfied."

Ogilvie nodded thoughtfully, looking again at the fat body of the Rajah. That greasy little potentate would be satisfied with much less than the conquest of Hyderabad and the British Raj: his bodily needs would suffice. In any case, there was a contradiction in basis, for His Highness had insisted that he was friend of the Raj, and he had sounded genuine. He didn't appear to be a man of much will or character; the danger, and quite clearly the architect of the plan, was General Rajeshwar Acharya, who was a horse of a very different colour. The Rajah, simple fellow, would have been easy enough to manipulate . . . Taking some wine offered by one of the serving women, Ogilvie made an attempt to lead the former *Risaldar*-Major into indiscretion, asking oblique questions as to his tactical plan and the strength of his forces currently massed between the Tunga Bhadra and the Kistna Rivers. Rajeshwar Acharya was in an expansive mood; but even so was not forthcoming militarily. All that emerged was that he had men disposed along the Kistna River's southern bank and that already in some sectors there had been an advance across the river.

"Suppose," Ogilvie said carefully, "your men happen to come upon any British troops. Will they attack?"

The General gave no immediate answer, and when it did come it was evasive, and with a lurking threat behind it. "You speak of possible British units. You shall, I think, speak further of that, Captain sahib."

Ogilvie shrugged. "I know little. In any case, the former *Risaldar*-Major of the Bengal Lancers will scarcely expect a British officer to give away information . . . will he?"

"You cannot shame me, Captain sahib. My ties with the Raj are cut, and cut finally. There is no going back." The General, seeing that His Highness was about to be lifted to his feet by his attendants, also rose. Ogilvie followed suit.

The Rajah was grinning at him, almost lasciviously, a leer more than a grin. Ogilvie felt distinctly uncomfortable.

The Rajah's leer widened to a smile. He lifted his hands to his ears. "Flap, flap," he said.

Ogilvie once again indulged in the harmless charade of being an elephant. At his side Rajeshwar Acharya spoke in a native dialect, one not so dissimilar from Pushtu and one that Ogilvie was able to follow enough to get its drift. The General said, "Your Highness, there are other matters—"

"Flap, flap."

"More important matters, Your Highness."

"So, yes. British officer sahib is good. Tonight we shall be happy."

"Your Highness, tonight is for other things."

"Not."

"Your Highness, I must insist. The British officer sahib must have knowledge helpful to us, and I must find it out."

The Rajah's face fell and he began to look obstinate. There was a stream of rapid talk, much of it, Ogilvie believed, abusive. The pith of it was that Rajeshwar Acharya was the son of a pig and that military matters must wait for morning's light to illuminate them. The General, growing angry, was forced to shout his master down.

"Your pardon, Your Highness, but you seem to have forgotten that at this moment my soldiers are outflanking the British to the eastward after crossing the Kistna. Much danger may await them from formations in the north—and I must know the facts. If I am not given the chance to find them out, I cannot lead Your Highness's army."

He stood before the Rajah, tall, powerful, implacable, arms folded and eyes steadfast beneath his turban. The Rajah wilted, tears came to his eyes and ran down his puffy cheeks, and he shook a fist at his army commander. Then he turned away and, helped by his attendants, left the apartment. Rajeshwar Acharya relaxed his stance and turned to Ogilvie. "Now, Captain sahib," he said, speaking courteously enough, "to your apartment. There we shall talk. I think you will be helpful, and I trust you will be fast. Time is short. As we go to your apartment, you will be good enough to ponder. I wish to know the full extent of your British and Indian Army commitment in the state of Hyderabad, and what your dispositions are between the Kistna and the Nizam's capital."

*   *   *

In his room, the window of which was uncurtained and showed a night sky filled with low-slung stars, Ogilvie was told to sit, while Rajeshwar Acharya brought up another chair and sat opposite him with folded arms. There was an armed guard on the door outside, and in the room, with his back against the door, stood a strongly-built Negro stripped to the waist and carrying a many-thonged whip made of leather and with lead weights attached to the end of the thongs. Almost as soon as Ogilvie had sat down, the General ordered him to get to his feet again.

"Go to the window, and look out."

"I already have, earlier."

"Go again. It is night now, and different."

Ogilvie shrugged and obeyed. He looked down to the many lights guttering in the old city, dim but widespread, some of them moving—flares, probably, being carried by the Rajah's soldiers on patrol duty. Somehow night and the pin-points below made the drop seem much longer and the city more dangerous, as indeed it would be to the wayfarer subject to attack at any moment from evil men who could in a twinkling glide back to the anonymity of the smelly alleys and the doorways of the stinking hovels with their beds of dirty, louse-ridden matting. At his side Rajeshwar Acharya said, "Escape is out of the question. Even if you could survive the drop, you could not get away from the city. Do you realise this?"

"Yes."

"Then help yourself by talking, Captain sahib. Sit down again."

Ogilvie went back to the chair, with the General once again seated opposite. "We have many, many ways of persuasion, Captain sahib. There are the lighted tapers to be set beneath the finger-nails, there are the thumb-and ankle-screws, there is the water torture—the drip into the nose with the mouth held shut which gives the sensation of drowning—and you see the whip."

Ogilvie nodded. "I see the whip."

"You would not wish to feel it."

"Of course not."

"You will not have seen a man flogged? When I first entered the service of the Raj, which was very many years ago, flogging was still a punishment for common soldiers in the British Army. Me, I have seen men strapped to the field gun wheels, the limber wheels, spread-eagled and flogged until the flesh peeled in strips and the blood spurted." The General paused. "No, you would not wish that, Captain sahib, and it is not necessary that you should. Help us and you will be spared, and you will be richly rewarded and live a life of ease in Indian service."

Ogilvie saw a possible way through. "I know almost nothing that can help you—you may not believe that, but it's the truth." He hesitated. "You've not asked where I came from nor what I was doing. Perhaps you should know."

The dark eyes seemed to bore into him. "Then tell me, Captain sahib, and we shall not lose time."

"I come from Ootacamund, the headquarters—"

"Of Southern Army—this I know. Go on. If you come from Ootacamund, you have much to tell."

"No." Ogilvie shook his head and began to sweat. About to tell the truth, he could only hope for belief: at least the telling of the truth usually sounded convincing. "I was told nothing, and for a good reason: I was in Ootacamund to be Court Martialled . . . then I was sent north by train, and left the train after an attack by bandits. This is the truth. If you are able to check, it will be substantiated."

"And the Court Martial charge, Captain sahib?"

"Cowardice," Ogilvie said steadily. "I am Captain James Ogilvie of the—"

"Ogilvie!"

"Yes. My father is the Northern Army Commander at Murree—"

"Yes, I have heard of him. Cowardice! Such a father, to have such a son!"

"You needn't rub it in. I can't face him again. I can't face the Raj. I can't face the whip. Your past is similar, except that you weren't guilty of cowardice. I think you'll understand." Ogilvie put his face in his hands. "I'll tell you the little I know."

Fourteen

THE PLOY SUCCEEDED beyond Ogilvie's hopes: it was accepted that he had spoken the truth. All the circumstances acted in support: the curious clothing, the uniform stuffed unceremoniously into the Gladstone bag, even the rescue from the bandits. Rajeshwar Acharya was at first inclined to think he could be a plant, a spy, but recognised that his story, if false, was too clumsy a one to succeed in drawing wool over anyone's eyes. It was so outlandish it had to be true. Ogilvie in fact revealed nothing that could be of particular use to the enemy, telling only what must be known, or at least strongly suspected and therefore already being countered: that there was a British advance south upon the Kistna in support of the Nizam. He had indeed already heard Rajeshwar Acharya's statement to the Rajah that the Rangapore soldiers were marching to outflank the British.

"I can't indicate where they'll be now," he said. "But I can take you to a point that'll cross their line of march."

"What use will this be, Captain sahib?"

"Well, you'll be able to engage, won't you? You spoke of outflanking—"

"Yes. Our outflanking force will march north upon Hyderabad, so—"

"You won't want to leave an army in your rear."

"This is true." The General pulled at his moustaches. "An intact army, ready placed to cross the Kistna perhaps, even to attack Rangapore? You think this?"

"I've no idea," Ogilvie answered with honesty, "but that could happen, I imagine. It's a risk to be considered, anyway."

"It shall be considered." Rajeshwar Acharya got to his feet at once, his decision made. "We ride for the Kistna immediately, and you shall come."

"And the Rajah?"

"His Highness need not be brought from his pleasures." The General motioned for the door to be opened; as he and Ogilvie went through he gave an order to the guard outside. The man fell in behind Ogilvie with his rifle held ready. In the great main hall below the General called to an attendant and sent him for his Chief of Staff. The latter, arriving quickly, was given orders to prepare two squadrons of lancers and to provide a good horse for the Captain sahib. For his part the Captain sahib was apprehensive about riding in a kilt rather than trews, but politely refused the General's offer of jodhpurs; he preferred that there should be no possibility of mistake when he rejoined the British line, and Rajeshwar Acharya was satisfied with his comment that tradition and his regimental background utterly precluded the wearing of a full-dress doublet with jodhpurs.

"The British are mad," the General said with a sigh, "but it is a madness that the past years have acustomed me to. Ride, if that is your wish, with the skin flayed from your bottom as truly as if the whip had been used!"

*   *   *

Hooves clattered across the courtyard and through the gateway into the city. Men scattered from the arrogance of the riders' progress beneath the fluttering guidons on the lances. Both squadrons consisted of big men, warriors to a man, with faces made for battle and the cut and thrust of steel. Once clear of the filth and stench of the drains of Rangapore, Rajeshwar Acharya passed the order to advance at the gallop, and they began to thunder along the track, heading out north-eastwards for the Kistna River. They faced a ride of some thirty miles before they would strike the river, and from there Ogilvie intended to lead the squadrons

172

eastward until they were more or less in the vicinity of the Royal Strathspey's point of aim as last known to him.

After that, what?

It was a question to be pondered, and Ogilvie, riding between a strong personal escort whose presence indicated that the General was taking no chances, racked his brains. His first objective remained as before: to make contact with British troops. He could pass on the information that the Rajah's main army was outflanking to the east and striking up for the Nizam's capital city; but by this time the British could well know this for themselves, and anyhow it was not of itself enough to help his case or to bring himself glad welcome from Lord Brora. More, much more, had to be achieved; but for now he was forced to settle for taking all events as they came. India was as ever India, the great sub-continent where the outlandish was the commonplace, the unlikely was the norm, and the utterly impossible kept on happening . . . in the meantime Ogilvie found himself responding to the thrill of the night ride, the dedicated gallop of his companion warriors, the wind in his face, the power of the horse beneath him; though the ride was spoiled by the terrible rawness of his posterior parts. He was, he knew, virtually glued to the saddle with blood. En route they passed bivouacked concentrations of the rebel army, all with strong picquets out even though they were as yet within the bounds of the Rajah's domain. There were some of the seven thousand elephants in compounds, stirring fretfully in the night as they heard, with those flap-flap ears, the sounds of fast horsemen. They passed gun-parks filled with all manner of artillery, ancient pieces that with luck would explode in flying fragments upon their own gunners the moment the firing lanyards were pulled, but many modern field guns as well, visible in clear moonlight, that had obviously been taken in battle or stolen from the military arsenals of the Raj together with their piled ammunition, both shells and cordite charges. The boasts of the Rajah had been no idle ones: he had the power, assuming the expected

173

degree of support that would join him as soon as he was seen to be successful, to flutter the dovecots from Calcutta to Cape Comorin; and that was to say the very least.

The last of the encampments, one containing what seemed to Ogilvie to be roughly the equivalent of a British brigade with artillery and cavalry, was entered by the General, who pulled up his lancers in a bath of sweat and heavy breathing from the all-out ride from Rangapore. Riding into this camp at a walk, Rajeshwar Acharya turned to Ogilvie.

"The Kistna is now within a stone's-throw. We shall ride on supported by the soldiers you see here. We still have some hours of darkness, time enough to march again by the dawn."

"You intend to cross the river, General sahib?"

"Yes. You shall stay here in this camp—"

"You'll need me with you, surely?"

The native leader shook his head. "Not so. You will indicate upon the map where the British force will be marching. That will be enough. The Kistna is fordable close to the camp, and that is where I shall cross, and then attack from the flank. That is, if it is to be assumed, as it is, that the British are marching along a track to the east of us here. You shall study the map, then we shall know." Rajeshwar Acharya returned the salutes of the guard, and then, riding forward, spoke once more to Ogilvie. "If your information should prove false, Captain sahib, you will die before the succeeding dawn."

*   *   *

The previous morning, after Masefield's brigade had reached the Kistna and the battalion commanders had been summoned by the Brigadier-General, there had been acid words spoken by Lord Brora.

"We're here on a fool's errand, sir. I dislike being made a fool of." He waved a hand around the empty landscape, the equally empty river. The gesture was elaborate and contemptuous. "No enemy. Not even a hostile animal to engage!"

Masefield glared, as angry himself as Brora. "Then what, may I ask, would you propose to do?"

"I? I, sir, propose to withdraw my regiment immediately."

"Do you indeed? You may propose, Brora, but you shall not execute. I am in command here, not you."

"In command of an empty battlefield, a place of no value because the damned rebel has taken himself elsewhere! A whole brigade tied up when it may be needed in other theatres. Do you propose to sit and wait, my dear sir?"

"I think I have no alternative," Masefield snapped. "My orders were for the Kistna, and I have arrived—"

"Then you mean to await more orders?"

"Yes."

Brora gave a loud sniff. "As I thought. My ideas are different, as it happens. I consider it imperative that we should seek out the rebel and attack him—"

"If we remain here, we're likely to draw his fire, Brora. He'll not neglect a brigade upon the Kistna. You will get your action then, you may be sure."

"Poor tactics, sir. Defence is always at a disadvantage in open country—"

"We shall have our backs to the Kistna—"

"Which is no *wall* in my eyes, sir. The best method of defence is attack. In war one needs dash and daring, sir, dash and daring! If I were in your shoes I would split the brigade and march to east and west of the route by which we came south . . . and see what is to be seen, fight what is there to be fought. Remember the dead we passed, sir, the dead of Skinner's Horse." Brora once again swung an arm through the air. "The enemy is quite clearly *somewhere* in the vicinity, is he not?"

"It doesn't follow. The attack on Skinner's Horse is history by now, with time enough elapsed for the rebels to have put many miles between—"

"Oh, stuff-and-nonsense, sir!" Lord Brora rose in his

175

stirrups, his colour high. "If you'll not fight, I shall! I shall withdraw my battalion and make a foray to the west, along the river, towards the rebel stronghold in Rangapore—and strike at the enemy's heart!" He gave a snort. "By God, it'll make a fine story in Secunderabad, will it not—and in Ootacamund, and in Calcutta . . . how a single battalion of Scots cut down the rebel, while the Brigadier-General sat on his damn arse upon the Kistna, whistling into the wind for orders!"

"You—you—" Masefield's face was mottled and he struggled for speech.

"A very good day to you, sir." Lord Brora gave an ironic bow, a swinging salute, turned his horse's rump towards Brigade, and rode back to his battalion. He was smiling to himself as he went, and he went, as usual, with an arrogant swing of his shoulders. There was no movement from Brigade to stop him and he was almost chortling as Andrew Black rode forward to greet his return.

"Are we to remain here, sir?" Black asked.

"By God we'll not," was Brora's answer, crisply given, "though Masefield *says* we will!"

Black sucked in his breath. "You've refused his orders, Colonel?"

"As he believes, yes. But there are other methods, Captain Black. Let us have patience, and await some back-tracking from our Brigadier-General, shall we?"

"Do you suppose—"

"I suppose, my good Black, that he will be sore from my metaphorical shot up his backside, but that reflection will show him the wisdom and truth of what I told him."

Brora turned and rode away, leaving the Adjutant pulling at his moustache in some perplexity. As it happened, orders from Brigade did not come as quickly as the Colonel had expected they might; when they did come, they were indecisive: the force was to remain *in situ* temporarily while patrols were sent out to make probes along the river and into the areas to the north-east and north-west. In the meantime,

176

the men were to be rested in bivouacs in the care of picquets. Brora was furious and made no bones about it.

"Masefield's taken in what I said and sees I was right, but he hasn't the damn guts to act upon it. I shall not wait all day for him to make up his mind!"

With the customary speed of the bush telegraph, the purport of the Colonel's words spread round the bivouacs, reaching every man in the battalion and those of the other battalions as well. Opinions were mixed: many were for Brora, who was seen to be keen to finish the job; many were not, realising that a split in the command could bring only evil with it and give advantage to the rebel waiting somewhere in the wings. Cunningham, old woman or not in the Colonel's view, continued doing what he had always done: sounding out the feeling unobtrusively, gauging the likely reaction of the rank and file if the Colonel should cock a final snook at Brigade and lead the regiment to action on its own. The Adjutant, knowing Cunningham and knowing Lord Brora's impatience with him, took pains to encounter the Regimental Sergeant-Major as if by chance and at some distance from the Colonel.

"Well, Mr Cunningham?"

Cunningham understood what was being asked of him. He said, "The feeling's fifty-fifty, sir, I'd say. Or perhaps just slightly against."

"Against the Colonel?"

Cunningham's look said the Adjutant was guilty of an indiscretion. "I'd not say that, sir. Against rumour, sir, maybe."

"Oh, we'll not make a play upon words, Mr Cunningham," Black said with an impatient frown. "Tell me—how does the split run?"

"The younger men, sir, they're in favour of independent attack." Cunningham's euphemism for "disobedience of orders" brought a faint smile to Black's sallow, constipated-looking face. "They're inexperienced enough not to see what the older ones see too well, sir."

177

"And that is?"

Unemotionally Cunningham said, "Captain Black, sir, I think you know what I mean. Independent action of the kind rumour speaks of—that gives a regiment a bad name, sir. I think you'll agree, sir, on reflection."

Black nodded, a hand straying over the deep lines of his face. He knew, and he agreed. Individual officers could sometimes do insane things and get away with it, could often, indeed, improve their career prospects in so doing. A regiment, never. And the Colonel was the regiment. If the Colonel disobeyed orders on a regimental scale, if he should lead his regiment counter to command and authority, then the regiment suffered afterwards, the more especially if the men—all the men—should not put the best foot forward. Give a dog a bad name . . . and it was easy enough for a regiment to fall from grace! When it did, life became unpleasant for all concerned. Obscure postings, postings to the hell stations reserved for bad battalions—postings to such places as Multan, a "punishment station" where the day temperature could climb to 125 degrees in the shade; or they could be sent home in something approaching disgrace. These would be sad endings to hard years of service in India. The Royal Strathspey must suffer no bad name on account of its Colonel's indiscretions—its *acting* Colonel's. Among other aspects, it would be hard upon Lord Dornoch, waiting to take up his command again . . . Black, who felt that enough had now been said, nodded in dismissal, and the Regimental Sergeant-Major, saluting, turned about and marched away.

Black was in a quandary. He felt deeply that Cunningham was right, but Lord Brora was a hard man to deal with, an impossible one to argue with or to deflect. Black felt he was in a cleft stick: Cunningham had uttered the warning which afterwards could scarcely be denied. In a sense he had been foolish to ask. Black compressed his lips and hurried away to begin chasing the company commanders; the orders from Brigade had been for rest, but rest did not mean idleness and

Black hated seeing the men idle. There was much that could be done: the cleaning and polishing of equipment and arms among them. Black, as he spoke to the various officers, kept his senses alert. There was a curious reserve in the air; the NCOs looked glum. The battalion was not well. There was something extra to all that Cunningham had said: there was a lack of confidence in the Colonel's ability to make the right decisions.

*   *   *

A little before the sun went down the sky a runner came from Brigade to the battalion commanders: nothing had been reported by the returning patrols except in the sector westerly along the Kistna, where some native soldiers had been briefly spotted on the south bank before beating a retreat. That apart, the whole area seemed to be empty; and they were now out of communication with Secunderabad: the field telegraph line, laboriously laid by the sappers on the march, had been cut before the high command had come up with any orders following upon receipt of Masefield's information. Thus the Brigade-General intended to remain in bivouacs and wait developments. It was obviously possible an attack might be mounted from the west and full vigilance was to be maintained throughout the night with strong picquets posted around the perimeter of the bivouacs. There would be advanced scouts, to be provided by the Bombay Infantry; but the extended patrols were to be withdrawn.

"Why?" Brora demanded of Black, truculently.

Black shrugged. "I don't know, sir. I would suggest that perhaps the Brigadier-General wishes to draw the rebels on to engage the main body—"

"And not be put off by patrols?"

"It's likely, I think."

Brora swore. "They can't think we're bloody fools. They'll suspect a trap—it's normal to extend patrols. And what about that damn field telegraph? If the line's been cut, that means the damn rebel's outflanked us to our rear!"

179

"Not necessarily, Colonel. It could have been cut by bandits."

"Well, it could have been, but I doubt it." Brora strode up and down for a while, muttering to himself as the sun fell below the horizon and sent splendid colours shooting across the darkening sky. His footfalls were loud in the silence, somehow ominous, providing almost the only sound apart from the occasional cry of a bird or animal beyond the range of the bivouacs. Black felt strongly that the night was to prove a bitter one, that Brora's mind was preparing for the casting of the die. He was not far wrong. After some minutes of his solitary march, Brora came up to the Adjutant and halted, breathing hard. His voice seemed slurred, almost as though the whisky bottle was responsible, as he spoke.

"Damn Masefield. Brigadier-General or no . . . if he thinks I'm going to lie here in damn bivouacs to be slaughtered by rebels emerging from the dark . . . by God, Black, he must think again!"

"You'll ask him to change his mind, sir?"

Brora gave a jeering laugh. "No, he'll not do that, he's too damn stubborn! I've decided to act on my own."

"Is that wise?" Black was unable to prevent the words that provoked the tirade.

"Wise my arse. Where's wisdom? In bloody Parliament, in the universities, that's where wisdom is! Cissies the lot of 'em. Do nothing but talk and go to old women's bun fights. They can kiss my arse. I am Lord Brora. I fight, not talk. All officers and senior NCOs to report at once."

"Colonel, I—"

"Orders, Captain Black. Don't stand there staring, man. See to it immediately."

*   *   *

Rajeshwar Acharya rode along the front rank of his rebel army imperiously, for all the world like the old Duke of Cambridge reviewing his troops at Aldershot. Ogilvie, for one fanciful moment, almost expected Her Majesty Queen Victoria to appear in her carriage, all ready to take the salute as her regiments marched past to the sound of the fifes and drums. The array was massive: the cavalry champed in the van of the forthcoming advance, the horses rearing, keen to be away into the night as it began to approach the dawn. Behind them stood the infantry, rank upon rank, line upon line, regiment upon regiment, armed with all manner of weapons from modern rifles to *jezails* and muskets, some of them so antique that they had to be primed with flash and pan and ramrod. There were grenadier companies with grenades and curiously-fashioned bombs, there were artillery batteries with field guns and even mountain guns, the latter not yet assembled but their parts dangling around the bodies of their carrier mules. There were howitzers, Maxims, Gatlings; and there was the heavy artillery with its elephant-drawn batteries in rear of the infantry. The elephants were resplendently warlike, their great ivory tusks tipped with steel, their foreheads protected with massive shields, more steel to act as breastplates, with chain armour burnished bright to hang down the trunks and cover the backs and sides; their warrior *mahouts* were also covered in chain mail and were armed to the teeth with rifles, bayonets, knives and daggers. Immense, slow-moving with great limbers behind them, there was something magnificent even in their very obsolescence; but once action had been joined, they would be removed from their duties and replaced by the more phlegmatic bullocks against any necessity to shift the batteries. Now, drawn up for the march, they looked immovable and impregnable, monolithic in the moonlight, a sight to terrify.

His inspection complete, the rebel General rode back to where Ogilvie was being held under guard.

"A change of mind, Captain sahib. You shall come with us."

"Why the change?"

The General smiled. "Do you fear action?"

Ogilvie, whose first instinct was to deny any fear, checked himself in time. As a coward he had come, a coward he must now remain. Rajeshwar Acharya laughed, an insulting sound, and said, "Cast out fear. You will not be asked to bear arms! But I prefer, on reflection, to have you with me. You may have a use."

"A hostage, General sahib?"

"It is possible. The son of the General commanding at Murree—who knows? Siva the Great God, Siva the Destroyer of Life, he will give the answer, and you shall ride at my side until he gives it." Rajeshwar Acharya gestured at one of his retinue, and a tinny bugle sounded briefly. The General, surrounded by his personal staff and with Ogilvie under a strong escort, rode to take up his position in the lead of the soldiers. When he was ready another bugle sounded out and a volley of shouted orders came. Without music the great parade marched out for the Kistna amid a clop of hooves, the heavy rumble of the guns and limbers, the tramp of feet and the rattle of fixed bayonets, the very sound of war, the earth itself seeming to shake and tremble to the massive footfalls of the gun-elephants as they put their shoulders to the traces. They were soon at the Kistna and into its waters at the ford. Formation was remarkably well maintained throughout the crossing, and Ogilvie, who had looked upon the ford as one place where he might well be able to break away from his escort, found this impossible. The horsemen kept close and alert, one of the men holding his bridle throughout while three more kept him covered with their rifles. His hopes, reasonably high at first after his presence in the advance had been ordered, began to fade into a terrible foreboding that he was about to see a slaughter of British units. Back at the rebel camp the formation had appeared to be of brigade strength; it had grown into something like a division by the time they had moved out. There was dedication in the air, too, as though these warriors knew very well that all was at risk, that it was now or never. The hour had struck for them, perhaps before they had expected it, and they were at a high pitch of excitement and forward-looking. Such men always fought well and to the death; they must prove too much for Masefield's mixed brigade, assuming the latter had indeed reached the Kistna which, by Ogilvie's estimate, they surely would have done. On the other hand, it might be one of the other brigades they would encounter, another parallel force sent down from Secunderabad. On yet another hand it was entirely possible that no British force was in this sector, in which case Ogilvie's life would hang upon a very slender thread, a thread nicely set up for cutting by Rajeshwar Acharya's sabre. Ogilvie, who had never envisaged that his actions would send so vast a force against the advancing British, found himself hoping for the last of the three possibilities; his own death would be an insignificant thing as against the wiping out of an inferior British force as a result of what he had done . . .

Once upon the northern bank, the rebel army was turned easterly and the final phase of the advance began, the elephants crunching on, inexorably drawing their shards of destruction behind the infantry and cavalry. The General turned in his saddle to speak to Ogilvie, and dispelled the last of his hopes.

"I will tell you now, Captain sahib. It has perhaps crossed your mind that I am leading out a large force, too large a force perhaps, on the word of an officer of the Raj. But it is not your word alone, Captain sahib. Intelligence reached me at the camp that British patrols had been observed, riding from the east. When you spoke in Rangapore, it seems you spoke truly."

Ogilvie tried to sound pleased. "Am I, then, to go unguarded, General sahib?"

"No." The answer was final. Ogilvie wasn't too sorry for that; now, no parole had been given and his escape, if he could bring it about, would be his simple duty. He rode on with the advance, with the jingling harness and the rumble of the guns about him, the dry dust, raised by the marching feet and the horses, billowing to choke and stifle. Dawn had not

183

yet come, and there was still moonlight shining down in bright silver to touch the standards and guidons, the armour of the elephants and the dull metallic grey of the guns. It was a spendid sight, if not to British eyes, with a strong flavour of mediaeval romance about it that almost gave it unreality. But the men about Ogilvie were real enough, as were the many warlike sounds. And after a while Ogilvie began to pick up the faintest whisper of another sound, an unexpected one, coming down on a light breeze from ahead, the breeze that spoke of dawn about to break. He fancied that as yet no one else had heard it; then the sound increased, the savage and unmistakable sound that told the world of the coming of the Scots.

Rajeshwar Acharya, his face alight, turned towards Ogilvie. "The sound of the squealing pig!"

"The pipes and drums, General sahib."

"It is madness! You British never cease to astonish me with your madnesses."

Ogilvie, all his senses seeming to tingle, listened to the message of the pipes:

> March past the 42nd
> March past the forty-twa,
> March past the bare-arsed buggers
> Comin' frae th'Ashanti War.
> Some had kilts an' ithers hadnae—
> They were Heilan' johnnies raw!
> March past the 42nd
> March past the forty-twa,
> March past the bare-arsed buggers
> Marchin' doon the Broomielaw . . .

It was splendid, it was heartwarming, but Rajeshwar Acharya had got it right: Lord Brora must have taken leave of his senses to announce ahead the coming of his regiment. Nevertheless, the pipes and drums in their exultancy and their utter sureness of victory went straight to Ogilvie's central being. He was scarcely conscious of what he did, of his foolhardiness, his madness akin to Brora's, or of his luck in getting away with it. As the General and his Staff turned to give their orders, Ogilvie swung sideways, smashed his horse into that of one of his close escort, took the man completely by surprise, and seized his sabre. Twisting viciously, he wrested it free and at once sent it swinging round to his right. A head rolled in the dust beneath the horses' hooves, blood spurted, and the body fell to dangle from a stirrup. Ogilvie dug in his spurs and before anyone had reacted was away down the track ahead. Bullets zipped past, but he dodged them, heading first this way then that, closing the distance towards the van of the Royal Strathspey, now just in view as the night's darkness at last gave way to the first light of dawn.

Fifteen

THE REBEL SCOUTS were ahead, riding back fast to report. Keeping low on his horse's back, Ogilvie went like the wind between and below the singing bullets. Then the leading files of the advancing Scots opened fire as the pipers withdrew to the flanks and played on. Three of the scouts went down, whether from Scots bullets or fire from their own side was hard to determine. Ogilvie rode right through them and came out on the far side with no more than a couple of bullet scores across the fleshy part of his left arm. Then, as he came down on the Scots, the battle proper was joined. Ferocious fire was opened from the rebel army as the *jezails* went into action and, from the rear, the field guns sent their shells speeding over the heads of the cavalry and infantry. Ogilvie heard the order given for the Scots to stand fast, and then, reaching the van of the advance, now halted, he saw the astonishment in the eyes of officers and men as they recognised the dirt-streaked rider in the full dress uniform of their regiment. Brora seemed speechless; then disregarded Ogilvie as he attempted to rally the men, who were showing a disinclination to face so vastly superior a force. Ogilvie caught sight of the Regimental Sergeant-Major, his bulky figure moving at the double along the left flank of A Company.

"Mr Cunningham!"

Cunningham turned. "Aye, sir. I saw you, and glad I was to do so."

"Have we no support?"

"We're on our own, Captain Ogilvie, sir, by the Colonel's

order. You'll excuse me now." Cunningham turned and carried on towards the rear, shouting loudly down the line as the ranks broke and men began running, running anywhere, like rabbits, to dodge the bullets. Lord Brora rode down behind the Regimental Sergeant-Major, shouting himself hoarse, almost screaming at the colour-sergeants and corporals.

"Stand fast, you bastards, did you not hear my order? Cowards the lot of you! I'll have your hides for this afterwards if you live. Captain Black!" Brora stood in his stirrups, looking to right and left. "Captain Black, I say!"

"Coming, Colonel." Black's horse, whinnying in fear, dashed towards the Colonel.

"Captain Black, you will give the order to form square."

Black stared. "Form square, did you say, sir?"

"That's what I said. It's our only hope now. See to it at once."

Black saluted and turned his horse, bringing the animal up on its hind legs. He galloped away and began shouting the order at the company commanders and NCOs. The men seemed irresolute, some of them obeying the order, more running hither and thither aimlessly as the screaming shells landed and blew up with appalling effect. Ogilvie, himself almost stunned by the din and violence of the attack, was watching half a dozen Highlanders beating it to the right of the column when a shell landed among them. There was a brilliant flash and a roar, and a rising pall of smoke, and when the smoke cleared away there was just a hole in the dusty ground, and scattered remnants of bodies and field service uniforms. As Lord Brora turned his horse towards the enemy, who had not yet begun to close the Scots, his and Ogilvie's eyes met.

Brora's face was like a rock, though his eyes seemed to glow. "Well?"

"I've rejoined, Colonel."

"The devil you have. You're no officer of mine. Get out of my sight." Brora rode away; Ogilvie watched him go, and

187

was watching when a rebel bullet took the Colonel's horse. With a tearing scream the animal went down, lurching sideways. As Brora fell, his body gave a sudden contortion and as he hit the ground he lay still. Ogilvie ran towards him, keeping his body low, feeling bullets rip through his uniform. He was aware of Cunningham running up behind. Reaching Lord Brora, feeling for heartbeats, he found life. The Colonel was unconscious and there was blood at the base of his neck. As Cunningham came up breathlessly, they were joined by a medical orderly who busied himself with bandages and said that Surgeon Major Corton would attend as soon as he was able. Ogilvie looked up into Cunningham's face.

"Out for the count, Sar'nt-Major. Where's Captain Black?"

"Wounded also, sir, and badly. He'll not take command this day. I was coming to report to the Colonel, sir, and also to tell him the men are refusing orders. I'm making those reports to you now, sir."

"To me, Sar'nt-Major?"

"You're acting Colonel, sir. And you'd best act very quickly, sir. Things are none too good."

Ogilvie stood up. He looked around; the place was a shambles. Everywhere there seemed to be dead and dying and blood lay thick, with many of the men still milling about in some semblance of square formation while others, those who had started to run, were lying in such cover as could be found in open ground, having in most cases seen the futility as well as the danger of flight. But there seemed to be little stomach in any of them—and small wonder, Ogilvie thought, since the order had been to form square, a mode of battle-conduct that had served the British Army well enough under the great Duke of Wellington and many other distinguished generals before and since, but was now nothing more than a last-ditch stand against overwhelming odds. The odds were certainly overwhelming, but Ogilvie had no intention of accepting any last ditches.

"Mr Cunningham," he said, "I intend to split the battalion and move into the attack."

"Aye, sir."

"Send runners, if you please, to Captain Stuart and Captain Campbell. They're to take command of the half battalions, one to the right flank, the other to the left. They'll move five hundred yards north and south respectively, then westerly to take position along the enemy's flanks. When I give the word, they both attack simultaneously. It's the best we can do, and it gives us a fighting chance. All right, Mr Cunningham?"

"All right indeed, sir. I'll pass the word you're back—and in command. You'll see a difference, sir." The RSM saluted and went away at the double, shouting for runners. Under heavy fire that brought more and more casualties the battalion began to deploy to right and left. The stragglers moved in to join the others as the sergeants and corporals rounded them up. The word of Ogilvie's return went round like wildfire; the promised difference showed. A cheer went up, a cheer that almost overlaid the sound of gunfire. Savage Highland yells went up as the mustered companies moved away to the wail and beat of the pipes and drums, and there was a shout of triumphant joy from the ranks as something untoward took place in the enemy's rear: there was a tremendous explosion and chunks of metal and parts of bodies were seen to be flung sky-high in a spreading cloud, to drop back again upon the rebel force. A field gun, it appeared, had blown up, and the blast of the explosion, with the shell and charge in the barrel, could perhaps have caused the explosion of a whole battery; at all events, there was a significant drop in the volume of heavy fire. It also seemed to cause a minor panic in the rebel lines: there was much toing and froing of standards and guidons, a real mêlée that gave the Scots the opportunity to make good progress as the two half-battalions doubled into position for the flank attacks. As they had turned westward Ogilvie, with the pipes and drums behind him, had started to advance on the central line

189

between them, heading straight for the enemy. It was a bold advance that could be called foolhardy, but it was far from purposeless: the regiment's morale had slipped, and it was vital that it should be jacked back up again and firmly maintained thereafter. From the right flank the Regimental Sergeant-Major watched with his heart in his mouth, wishful to yell out to the officer not to be a bloody hero, yet forced to admit two things to himself: one, bravado was having its effect, and two, Lord Brora would very likely have been just as heroic without the proper effect and would somehow have contrived to turn it into an expression of scorn for less flamboyant hearts . . . In the meantime, Captain Ogilvie had the good Lord God with him—either that, or the luck of the devil! It seemed to spread to the pipers and drummers as well; they marched ahead unconcernedly just as though putting on a display at the regimental depot in Invermore in the Monadliath Mountains by Speyside, sending out loud and clear the martial strains, the tunes of Scotland's glory. Cunningham's heart swelled: it was as though all the Highland regiments were there with them, the Argyll and Sutherland, the Gordons, the Black Watch, the Cameron Highlanders, the Highland Light Infantry, the Seaforth. His Scots, that day, would fight after all.

*   *   *

As the men on the flanks began to come up level with the mass of the Rangapore soldiers, Ogilvie dropped back and lifted a hand to his bugler. The sound cut sharply through the swirling clouds of dust and the blowing gunsmoke from the heavy batteries. At once the half-battalions halted, spread out, dropped to the ground and opened a simultaneous and enfilading fire on both the rebel flanks. As the bullets tore and ripped into the bunched mass of natives, Ogilvie led the pipes and drums at the double to the right flank. The fire was intense on both sides, but now the native artillery was forced to accept two points of aim. The gaudy-uniformed natives fell in great swathes as the concentrated rifle and Maxim fire

190

swept into them, every single bullet finding, as it was bound to find, a target. In the Scots' hands the rifle-barrels grew hot with continual use, but Ogilvie groaned aloud as he saw his casualties mount. They were, after all, just one battalion and the odds were going to prove too much. He found Cunningham at his side, bleeding from the head.

"Take it easy, Sar'nt-Major," he said.

"I'll be all right, sir, it's no' but a glancing blow." The RSM gestured towards the enemy mass. "They're self-replacing, the buggers!"

"Like squares!"

Cunningham looked at him. "Sir?"

"Perhaps I was wrong. Squares can be effective. You can't always treat the old ways with contempt."

"No, sir. Not always. But this time you were *right*, sir! The men have responded because they knew that. Never say die, Captain Ogilvie, sir. There's fight in us yet."

"I don't want to lose the whole battalion, Bosom."

"No more do I, sir, as well you know. And I don't think that's going to happen. You know the undisciplined native levies, sir: no real stomach for being on the receiving end—the rebel especially. It's in his make-up. When he sees enough of his comrades die, he loses heart. Do you understand me, sir?"

Ogilvie nodded. "Yes. It's what I was relying on, but it doesn't seem to be happening."

"Give it time, sir. They'll break and run. I'll stake a dram on it."

"Done!" The fighting went on relentlessly, the rebel forces continuing to be badly cut up, heaped bodies lying everywhere and forming cover for the living. But only a matter of minutes later a change came: the break—but not the break to the rear prophesied by Cunningham. There was a sudden dash of horsemen towards the right flank, some score of them coming at a gallop towards the Scots, their guidons fluttering from the lances and Rajeshwar Acharya himself in the lead of the troop. They thundered down on the

191

sector where Ogilvie was crouching, the lance-points lowered to pierce and kill. Two of the Scots were taken and spitted like pigs before the concentrated rifle fire of the right-flank soldiers sent half the riders from their horses and turned the rest away. Amongst those who turned was Rajeshwar Acharya himself, and as he turned a lucky shot took his horse in the head and he was pitched forward, landing in a huddle on the ground. He seemed to be unhurt; as he picked himself up Ogilvie and Cunningham, with two privates, ran for him. The rebel leader drew a revolver and fired, and one of the privates fell dead; the other fired back, winging the native, and Ogilvie dived forward in a flying tackle for the legs. Rajeshwar Acharya went down again, flat and winded, and was at once covered by the rifles. Other men kept up a concentrated fire in the direction of the native troop, who withdrew at the gallop towards their own lines. Before they reached their lines, however, they pulled up and dismounted, and fired back upon the British, using their horses as cover.

Ogilvie pushed his revolver into Rajeshwar Acharya's spine, breathing hard. Lifting his voice in a carrying shout, he called to the native troop. "We have your General sahib prisoner, as you can see. He'll not be harmed so long as you do as I demand." He stopped, hoping that his English had been understood. "Do you hear me?"

There was a pause, then an arm was waved from the troop. "We hear."

"Good! Then hear more: there will be a parley, and all fighting will stop until it has been held. I ask that a high-ranking officer approach me under a flag of truce."

After another pause, another wave came. "Wait, and word will be ridden back. Your promise must be given that the General sahib will be safe."

"You have my word."

Another wave; a man mounted and rode back fast into the main body of the rebel army. The fighting continued; there was a longish wait, then the man was seen riding back. He pulled up his horse some fifty yards clear, and called, "Your wish is granted. A flag of truce will come. You will wait. Will you now cease firing?"

"When the flag of truce is seen. Not before."

Another wait; this time a short one. From the rebel ranks a party rode out at a canter, six men forming an escort under a white flag held high on a lance, and an officer in the centre. As the truce party appeared Ogilvie turned to Cunningham.

"Sound the Cease Fire, Sar'nt-Major."

"Aye, sir." Cunningham passed the order to a bugler. As the brassy notes blared out, the firing fell away and there was silence, a strange silence it seemed. Men remained in cover, waiting with fingers ready on the triggers, not trusting the word of the rebel. The truce party approached and Ogilvie, feeling a hand on his shoulder, turned to see Robin Stuart.

"What's the idea, James?"

"Isn't it obvious? I'll negotiate a withdrawal."

"Of the rebels?"

"Of course —"

"And us?"

"We stand our ground. There's plenty of support somewhere in the area north of the Kistna, Robin. If I send out patrols they're bound to make contact before long."

"Yes, I suppose you're right." Stuart blinked through the dust that caked his eyes. "After that, a march on Rangapore seems to be indicated!"

Ogilvie shrugged. "It'll be out of our hands by that time. Masefield'll be on the scene soon."

"And none too pleased with bloody Brora, I'll be bound!" Stuart looked across at Rajeshwar Acharya. "Your captured rebel looks like a real warrior, James."

"Late *Risaldar*-Major, Bengal Lancers," Ogilvie said briefly. "He'll swing on the end of a rope if he's caught here, and you can bet your own life he knows that as well as I do!"

Stuart lifted an eyebrow. "Your trump card, old man?" Suddenly he frowned. "Isn't this all somewhat irregular, basically? You're supposed to be under arrest still, I take it?"

"And now returned to your custody," Ogilvie answered, grinning. "But I warn you not to take your duty too seriously!" He turned away towards Rajeshwar Acharya to begin his negotiations. There was still a curious silence hanging over the opposing forces, a sense almost of a vacuum. High overhead the ubiquitous vultures hovered, not closing, seeming oddly to understand, in some uncanny fashion, that their time had not yet come. The sun was lifting higher now and the day's dry heat was setting in: the dead could not remain too long unburied. Ogilvie glanced at the impassive faces of the truce party and the officer who had come to take back his general's decisions: that general was in something of a cleft stick, and everything depended upon his personal courage and the degree of his loyalty to the Rajah of Rangapore. Ogilvie went straight to the central point.

"General sahib, we are certain to be joined by reinforcements shortly. Then your numerical superiority will be gone. In the meantime, you are in my custody and will be handed over to my Brigadier-General to face the justice of the Raj. You know what this means?"

Rajeshwar Acharya smiled, and drew a hand across his throat. "Death, Captain sahib."

"Yes."

"I have faced death many times," the rebel said carelessly.

"But not a dishonourable death."

"Where is the dishonour, Captain sahib? I fight for my own people, and there is no dishonour in that. I am the sworn enemy of the British Raj."

"But your ruler, your Rajah—he's a supporter of the Raj, General sahib, as he has said to me."

"Said is the important word, Captain sahib. His Highness says many things, and not all of them have a basis in fact."

"Then such being the case, General sahib, is your Rajah worth dying for?"

The black eyes searched Ogilvie's face, and then there was a scornful laugh. "No, he is not. When the time comes, it is I who will make the better Rajah of Rangapore." Slowly the

194

rebel lifted his hands to his ears and solemnly wagged them. "Flap, flap," he said, his tone heavily sardonic. "His Highness is but a child at heart." He waved an arm towards his waiting army. "You waste time, Captain sahib. My army is immense, and is more than adequate to beat you, reinforcements or not!"

"You sound convinced, but—"

"I am." The voice was quietly confident. "I would not have marched until I was certain of victory."

Ogilvie nodded. "Very well. I shall give you time to consider. I need scarcely remind you, *Risaldar*-Major, that the Raj never gives in to threats. No matter what you have said, you know that the Ninth Division from Secunderabad will be marching for the Kistna, reinforced by many supporting brigades detached from other commands. You and your army stand in much danger, and I advise you to withdraw at once."

Rajeshwar Acharya laughed in his face, insultingly. "If so much power is coming to join you, Captain sahib, why do you not merely detain my army to await its destruction?"

Ogilvie smiled and indicated the flag of truce. "I think your army *is* detained, General sahib, so long as the truce is observed. If it should be broken, you will die without waiting for the Raj."

"And thus achieve honourable death!" Rajeshwar Acharya lifted his voice to the truce party before anyone could stop him. "Away with the coward's flag—my orders are for war. Captain sahib, prepare to re-engage!"

The party from the rebel lines at once turned and cantered back to rejoin, the flag of truce still fluttering from the lance-point until they had reached safety. Ogilvie swung round on the Regimental Sergeant-Major. "Sound for action, Mr Cunningham."

"Sir!" Cunningham saluted, half turned away, then hesitated. "The hostage, sir. Do you—"

"Wait, Mr Cunningham. There may be a use for him yet. The bugles, if you please."

"Sir!" Cunningham passed the order to the bugler, and the soldier lifted the instrument to his lips. Then something that seemed like a miracle happened. As the action call sounded out, cleaving the air as gunfire started again from the rebels, a distant flash was seen from the north, then more flashes, and below them a rising cloud of dust. Cunningham seemed momentarily taken aback, uncomprehending; then he recognised the flashes for what they were. He called out, "A heliograph, sir! God be praised, sir, it's the bloody reinforcements!" He read off the message himself: "Report situation, sir."

Ogilvie had swung round and was looking towards the sun's reflected flashes almost in awe. "Tell them we're outnumbered and require immediate assistance," he said. Then, as the battalion signallers got busy the distant cloud of dust seemed to expand sideways and upwards, almost to explode. A cheer went up from the Scots as the relieving force was seen. Out from the dust, leaving it clinging to their tails as they outpaced it, stormed what looked in the field glasses like three full regiments of cavalry—a cavalry brigade, no less, with some sixteen hundred horses coming down at the charge. And away on the cavalry's flanks, one on either side, rode two brigades of the Royal Horse Artillery, adding six hundred horses and twenty-four heavy-calibre guns to the onslaught. Helmets were flung into the air from the Scots line as the artillery brigades, thundering down, closed the range and the horses swung the guns and limbers right and left and halted with the field pieces in position for Action Front. Almost within seconds, they were firing; to the north of the opposing forces the plain seemed to sprout great plumes of white smoke, and then the express-train whistles of the shells were heard as the projectiles were flung through the air to drop and explode and shatter in the dead centre of the rebel mass.

Sixteen

AS THE GUNS wrought their shrieking havoc, as men died horribly and bloodily from fire and metal splinter, the cavalry brigades, temporarily halted, moved in. The drummers beat a long roll that swept down between the explosions as a sound of vengeance; the lances dipped, flashing silver in the early morning sunlight, and the mass of horses hurtled forward at a stretch-gallop, hooves pounding the dust to bring it up in clouds through which the blancoed gauntlets of the troopers showed like angels' wings. As they closed they cut with the slicing blades of the sabres and spitted men with the lances or fired carbines point-blank from the saddle. Panic took the rebel horde by the throat: with their general in the hands of the Raj, their stomach for the fight began to shrink. There was a maddened trumpeting from the elephants, now detached from the guns and herded into a makeshift compound. Guard ropes parted, stakes flew from the ground, and the elephants moved en masse, plunging on huge feet away from the noise and the close exploding shells. The panic, having started, grew worse: the power and vengeance of the Queen-Empress was too manifestly seen and the discretion of flight in the wake of the fast departing elephants was now seen as the better prospect. The native army broke, its units streaming to the rear, yelling, screaming as the pursuing guns and lances bit and bit again. It was a bloody business, but within the hour the battle had flickered to its end; and a Major-General rode down upon the weary Scots.

"Who's in charge here, where's your Colonel?"

Ogilvie came to attention and saluted. "Lord Brora's wounded, sir. I am acting in command."

The Major-General stared with immense curiosity. "I see. I've known Scots regiments before now, but by God I've never seen any of 'em fight in full dress! Comes expensive, doesn't it? What's your name?"

"Ogilvie, sir."

"Ogilvie?" The Major-General was clearly surprised; no doubt he would have had the reports. Possibly he understood; in any case he offered no comment but, after a close scrutiny of Ogilvie, cleared his throat and said, "Well, you've done a good job, by the look of it—holding that mob with a battalion is no mean feat. At a cost, of course." He looked around at the dead, far too many of them, lying huddled in the dust. "A count of casualties, Captain Ogilvie, and a nominal roll, then burial parties. My medicos and *doolie-wallahs* are at your doctor's disposal."

"Thank you, sir."

"After that . . ." The Major-General paused. "You're from General Masefield's brigade—why is your battalion detached?"

The question was only to be expected, but was nevertheless embarrassing. Ogilvie got round it. "I'm not fully aware of all the circumstances, sir. I rejoined only a couple of hours or so ago." He added, "From Rangapore."

"Rangapore, by jove! I think, Captain Ogilvie, you'd better explain in rather more detail, hadn't you?"

*   *   *

Major-General Corcoran preferred not to know too much about Ogilvie's self-release from arrest: not his affair, he said, and he had no wish to be forced to place Ogilvie back in custody. A blind eye and a deaf ear would be turned: Corcoran was very human and in addition had heard tales of Lord Brora when stationed at home. He voiced no criticism of Brora, but his very forbearance told its own story. He questioned Ogilvie closely about the city of Rangapore and was at the end of his interrogation when a sergeant approached, saluted Ogilvie, and reported wooden-faced that Rajeshwar Acharya had, in the heat of the artillery and cavalry attack, evaded his escort and seized a revolver from the body of a dead officer.

"Shot himself through the head, sir."

"Dead?"

"Aye, sir, as a doornail."

Ogilvie caught the Major-General's eye, read the message, and gestured to the sergeant to move out of earshot. "No action against the escort, sir?" he asked Corcoran.

"It's your affair, but I think not. What would be gained? For an ex-*Risaldar*-Major, it's the best way, don't you think?" He paused. "The question of a guide through the native state to the rebels' HQ — you can cope, I imagine?"

"Yes, sir."

"Well, that's where I intend marching as soon as the burial parties are finished." Corcoran added that he was using his rank to extract Ogilvie in the capacity of guide attached to his staff, but would not press the battalion itself out of Masefield's command unless its acting commanding oficer was willing and agreeable.

"I'm going in to finish the job, Ogilvie," he said. "I have the strength and now's the time to take advantage of a rout. Well?"

"The battalion'll want to finish the job, too, sir."

The Major-General nodded in approval. "Well said, and so they shall." As he passed the outline of his intentions for the march, another report came in: Brigadier-General Masefield was approaching from the east with the remainder of his brigade. Soon after this, Masefield rode in, looking for Brora's blood. He saluted the Major-General.

"And you are who, sir?"

"Corcoran, commanding an independent force from Secunderabad, marching parallel to yourself. I heard gunfire, and swung to investigate."

"Lucky you did."

Corcoran scratched his jaw and grinned. "Oh, I don't know! Young Ogilvie was giving a pretty good account of himself."

"Ogilvie?" Masefield was as astonished as the Major-General had been. "I'll be damned! What's been going on?" He turned on Ogilvie. "I didn't recognise you at first, young man. You'll kindly explain—"

"All right, Masefield, he's explained to me. Leave it with me, there's a good chap." Corcoran added his proposals for carrying the battle into Rangapore city. "Will you join me, Masefield?"

"Gladly! There's no sign of an enemy eastwards." Masefield eased his Wolseley helmet from his forehead. "Where is your Colonel, Captain Ogilvie?"

Ogilvie was about to answer when there was a diversion: a stretcher-party approached, carrying Brora himself and bound for the field ambulance section attached to Corcoran's column. Brora looked white and sick and the red blankets that enfolded him were wet with blood; his eyes were closed but as he was borne abreast of the group he opened them and stared about. The eyes focused on Ogilvie, and there was an accusing look. Brora's voice was strong enough as he uttered.

"The second time, Captain Ogilvie, and I shall see to it there won't be a third."

"Second time for what, Colonel?"

"Chestnuts picked out of the fire by the damn cavalry, that's what! I won't have my regiment always rescued by the cavalry, I tell you! As an officer in arrest, you had no right to the command in any case. I shall Court Martial every officer who permitted you to do so!"

"Does that include me, Lord Brora?"

Brora's eyes swivelled towards the Major-General. "Who the devil are you, sir?"

"Major-General Corcoran, who has in retrospect both permitted and condoned Captain Ogilvie's action."

"Balls to retrospect, sir," Brora said rudely. "And I don't give a damn fig for your rank. I am Lord Brora. *I* command the Royal Strathspey, and I order that Captain Ogilvie be returned to arrest immediately and sent under close escort to Ootacamund where Sir Clarence Farrar-Drumm awaits him."

The Major-General, his face angrily flushed, turned his back on the *doolie*. Brora continued speaking; Masefield gestured at the *doolie-wallahs* to remove him. He was carried away protesting loudly: it was an embarrassing moment and yet a sad one. Brora was no hanger-back in action and in that respect was a good officer. Corcoran, looking troubled as well as angry, caught Masefield's eye. "Brigadier, I think you have a ready-made formula?"

"Yes, I have. As of the time he was wounded, Lord Brora was superseded in active command. In any case, he had disobeyed my orders, and I have yet to consider that."

Corcoran put a hand on Masefield's shoulder. "Read the Riot Act—that's my suggestion—rather than use too heavy a hand. He's been badly shot. He's always been a thorn in the flesh, but . . ." He threw up his hands. "I'll say no more." He turned to his Chief of Staff. "Runners to all commanding officers. The column is to be fallen in for the march on Rangapore. Have the scouts and picquets fully alert throughout. Captain Ogilvie?"

"Sir?"

"You still command your battalion. They've done splendid work today, and your pipes and drums will lead—with your permission, that is."

"Sir!"

"Carry on, then, Captain Ogilvie."

Ogilvie saluted and turned about, marching away to give his orders. Rejoining the battalion he found the officers and men eager for the advance. Pipe-Major Ross swelled out his chest with pleasure at the compliment paid by the Major-General, and lost no time in marching his pipes and drums to the head of the column behind the cavalry.

Ogilvie had reported to the Major-General that the rebels, according to Rajeshwar Acharya, had a force marching towards Hyderabad and outflanking the British advance by keeping to the east. The Major-General had taken this into account when formulating his plans; the Ninth Division, he had said, had moved down from Secunderabad to throw a cordon around Hyderabad city, and the rebels' outflanking army, now without reinforcements, would march straight into the guns. His own advance on the heart of Rangapore should prove the decisive blow, and the rebel army marching north would, in effect, find its base cut off behind it. In the meantime, with Ogilvie riding ahead of the column in his capacity of guide, Corcoran's horses, guns and men forded the Kistna in the same spot as Ogilvie had crossed in the night. The were signs en route of the rebel retreat: men and horses that had died of wounds and were already torn by the vultures' beaks, abandoned guns and limbers, trails of blood in the dust. At the ford more guns had been left, indicating a panic haste to get away. Ogilvie led the long, sweat-streaked column past the encampment where Rajeshwar Acharya had formed his army for the grand assault; this, too, was abandoned and there was every sign of a hasty evacuation reported by the infantry company detached by the Major-General to check the area: there was not a native to be seen.

"It's plain what's happened," Corcoran said, addressing Ogilvie who had joined him as they approached the deserted encampment. "They've all fallen back on Rangapore, seeking safety behind the walls!"

"The palace area won't hold them all, sir."

"Perhaps not, but I suppose the city is defensible?"

"A lot of it lies outside the walls, sir, the original walls of the old city."

"Susceptible to gunfire?"

Ogilvie grinned. "I'd not like to be an inhabitant, sir, under heavy bombardment!"

There was a nod. "A tinder-box indeed! All the same, I've no wish for unnecessary slaughter, just so long as the point's made that the Raj can't be rebelled against. That's what I'm here for, not to lead a punitive expedition." Corcoran added, "It's up to them entirely whether they resist us or not."

"I don't believe His Highness will resist for long, sir."

"No stomach for a fight?"

"He prefers filling his stomach from the flesh-pots, sir. He was being pushed by Rajeshwar Acharya."

The Major-General nodded. "As you reported earlier. We may be advancing into a nice, soft underbelly! How far to go now?"

"A little under thirty miles, sir."

"Well, I can't press the infantry any harder. It'll be almost two days' march for them as it is." Corcoran turned to his Chief of Staff. "Runners, if you please. I intend riding ahead with a regiment of cavalry and two horse batteries, the remainder of the column to march on behind me. I shall leave a spoor for them to follow. You'll come with me, Ogilvie."

*   *   *

The mounted advance-guard was swift: in just over four hours they had the city in view. Breasting some rising ground Ogilvie and Corcoran looked down on the close clusters of buildings, on the high old walls that surrounded the palace. The day's heat was intense and seemed, if only in anticipation as yet, to draw out all the smells of Rangapore as the cavalry and guns rode forward across the Indian plain. Corcoran was using his field glasses, as was Ogilvie: the city seemed like an anthill, crawling with life, and many pieces of heavy artillery could be seen in addition to the *jezails* and bayonets.

"Dangerous," Corcoran observed with a laugh, "more to themselves than us, I fancy! They'll bring the city about their ears if they open on us."

"While a few well-placed shells from us—"

"Exactly!" Corcoran was about to speak further when a bright flash was seen from the city, and a rumble was heard. Behind the flash a white wall crumbled in a rising cloud of dust, then the whine of the projectile was heard overhead, and, in rear, there was an explosion which brought up stones and earth to drop down on the riders. Corcoran brushed dirt from his uniform. Another shell came across, then another, the firing of each bringing down more of the close-set buildings. Corcoran was about to speak again when he gave a sudden exclamation, and ducked: the next shell had come uncomfortably low, and sped on to drop into the rear files of the cavalry. There were cries of agony from men and horses, and the clearing smoke showed a dozen dead or seriously wounded. Corcoran's mouth set into a thin line. "A lesson's needed. My compliments to the gunner Colonel. He's to bring his batteries to action immediately." He added, "Points of aim, the last gun that fired, and the palace itself."

A rider galloped towards the batteries of the Royal Horse Artillery. As the guns and limbers swung behind the horses, Ogilvie heard the strains of the cavalry canter, "Bonnie Dundee", playing a fast tempo as the hooves thundered in clouds of dust. Quickly the batteries took up position and opened, all guns together in a huge burst of noise and smoke. The group of officers watched the fall of shot: it was not possible to say whether or not any rebel guns had been destroyed, but amongst the explosions that rocked the city a high part of the palace building was seen to crumble and fall, smashing down upon the walls. Corcoran watched in silence; after three rounds from each gun he ordered the cease fire.

Peace descended, and quiet, a curious calm. "We wait, gentlemen," the Major-General said. They waited; there was no further firing from the city. Corcoran lowered his field glasses on the lanyard round his neck. "We shall advance, and see what happens next."

Orders were passed and once again the cavalry got on the move and the guns swung into line towards the city. Ogilvie eased the band of his collar, which was drenched with sticky sweat. Rangapore was something of an enigma yet: they could be advancing into a trap, into concentrated fire. There was little available cover outside the city; but Corcoran appeared unworried. He rode easily and in a relaxed posture, a smile playing about his lips as they approached. But as they closed to within some one hundred yards of the shanty-like outskirts, another shell came across from somewhere in the myriad alleys that criss-crossed each other like some great spider's-web; more dust rose over the city, and the shell burst immediately behind the advancing British cavalry. At the same time a man was seen waving his arms from a high tower, a man dressed in a flowing white garment like a priest.

The Major-General lifted an arm to halt the advance. "A shot across our bows, or anyway our stern," he said. "And a man with a message, I rather think."

The white-clad man was calling out, loudly, his voice clear in the still air following the explosion. "Come no closer or you will be blown to fragmentations. Where is your General sahib?"

Corcoran raised an arm. "I am the General," he shouted in carrying tones of authority. "In the name of Her Majesty the Queen-Empress, in the name of the Raj, I call upon you and your Rajah to surrender to me at once."

"His Highness will not surrender, General sahib."

"Then he's the one who'll be blown to your damned fragmentations," Corcoran replied. "Instant surrender, or my batteries open upon you—and remember this: I have strong forces marching behind me, with orders to take the city." He paused, then went on, "I do not come to kill unless killing is forced upon me. I come to persuade His Highness that to rebel against the British Raj does not pay and is doomed to failure. I say again, immense strength is ranged against you. If I open fire, your city will burn like the burning-ghats of Calcutta."

"We believe in our cause, and we have the strength of Siva, God of war, the destroyer."

"Have you indeed," the Major-General said in an aside. He raised his voice again. "I suggest a parley. Send an officer of high authority, and I will talk with him."

There was a pause; at a gesture from the Major-General, the horse batteries were moved, suggestively, a little closer to the sleazy outskirts, outskirts that were now empty of life as though everyone had been withdrawn into the heart of Rangapore. As the heavy rumble of the limber wheels and the creak of harness ceased again, the man on the tower called out, "Wait." Then he vanished.

"Siva seems not entirely strong enough," Corcoran observed, smiling. "I fancied he might not—but we shall see."

The wait was long-drawn-out. Men and horses grew restive; the sun started down the western sky, casting long shadows from distant hills and from the high buildings of the inner fortress. Corcoran walked his horse up and down, holding the reins lightly, his eye constantly upon the city and its guns where they were visible. At last the man in white appeared again on the tower, waved his arms, and called down to the waiting troops.

"An officer will not be sent, but Highness will parley with a British officer in his palace."

Corcoran scowled and pulled at his moustache. "Damn the bugger. Whoever goes in there takes his life in his hands, I rather think. I—"

He broke off: the man was calling again. "Highness wishes to be sent the Captain sahib who came before. Highness promises his safety."

Corcoran swore, then glanced at Ogilvie. "What's behind this, d'you think? Revenge? The Rajah will know by now you rejoined your regiment."

"I don't know what to think, sir. Except that . . ."

"Go on, Ogilvie."

"Yes, sir. As I told you, the Rajah's a trifle simple. I was able to humour him. He was really quite friendly."

"H'm." The Major-General pulled again at his moustache,

his face troubled. "I'll not order you to go in, Ogilvie. You're the very man who shouldn't, really. It'd be better if my ADC was sent."

"They ask for me, sir. I doubt if anyone else would do."

Corcoran gave him a keen, hard look, a searching look. "Do I take it you're willing?"

"Yes, sir. If I don't, there'll be slaughter."

"True. This isn't . . . by way of recompense, is it? Wiping the record?"

Ogilvie made no reply. Corcoran warned, "Because if it is, think again, Ogilvie. So far as it lies within my power to do so, I'll see to it that the record's regarded as clean already. Well?"

"Thank you, sir, but I'll go. I see it as my duty, since I've been named."

The Major-General nodded. "Very well." He called to the man on the tower, "The Captain sahib will come as you ask. You will treat him well and not harm him. If he has not returned within two hours, I shall open fire and destroy the city."

"Harm will not come to the Captain sahib. Now he is to walk forward alone, and wait at the nearest dwelling to where you are. An escort will come."

The man vanished again. Corcoran passed brief orders to Ogilvie, who saluted, dismounted, and walked ahead towards the city outskirts, into the long shadows.

Seventeen

IT WAS A naked feeling, one of so near and yet so far: the Major-General, the cavalry and the guns were within a stone's-throw of him but already he was as remote from them as if he had been on the summit of Mount Everest in the Himalayan snows. It would be a tough mission and he had been given little scope by Corcoran. He was to insist on total surrender and disarming and was to state the position of the Raj in unequivocal terms. If His Highness gave him a flat refusal, or if he should suggest terms, then Ogilvie was to return at once to report. He had been allowed one concession, and one only: he could strike a bargain, if the chance arose, over the women and children of the city. He could offer them safe conduct out before the bombardment started in return for his own safe deliverance back to the British lines.

After a wait of some twenty minutes, the escort was seen approaching from the mouth of an alley, six heavily-armed men of the Rajah's private army, men in colourful, ragged uniforms. Without a word being said on either side, the escort formed up around Ogilvie and he was marched into the alley, through the stink of the open drain, and past some of the damage caused by the guns, to the palace gates, and through them into the central courtyard and the great hall. In the courtyard he noted a good deal of fresh-looking rubble from a collapsed building.

*　　*　　*

He was received in audience by His Highness alone; the

208

Rajah, seated as before on his splendid golden throne, rose smiling to greet him and then the expected happened: the Rajah lifted his hands to his ears and said, "Flap, flap."

"Seven thousand flap, flaps, Your Highness."

"No, no. *Fourteen* thousand flap, flaps." The Rajah retreated back to his throne and motioned Ogilvie to sit on a mat by his feet. "Now not so many. Elephants they became terrified of big British guns."

"They ran, Your Highness?"

"So. Not come back. Many *mahouts* killed under tramping foots. *Mahouts* plentiful, but not elephants."

"The Raj has many elephants, Your Highness."

The small black eyes gleamed. "Raj would give elephants?"

No bargaining! "I cannot promise, Your Highness, but I will make representations for you."

"To good Queen Victoria?"

"Not directly."

"Then to Viceroy in Calcutta, perhaps. Would be good. When will this be?"

Ogilvie said, "When you recognise His Excellency's authority, Your Highness, and cease to make war upon the Nizam of Hyderabad, who, like you, is a good friend to the Raj."

"Not friend." The Rajah shook his head vigorously. "Not friend to British Raj."

"I understood you to say you were, Your Highness."

"Not now."

"That is a pity, Your Highness. It is also foolish, if I may say so. Your General sahib is dead, as no doubt you know. Have you other military leaders to take his place?"

"Yes," the Rajah answered petulantly.

There was a silence; then Ogilvie said, "But some shortage of elephants."

"Elephants have sad faces."

"And are mortal in battle, like men. Further battle would lose more elephants, Your Highness. And I think in any case

209

you would not wish to see the city of Rangapore, and this palace, destroyed by the guns of the Raj. I ask you to send me back to my General with word that you will fight the Raj no longer. I think that you never wished in your heart to attack the Empress of India . . . I think such ambitions were placed there by Rajeshwar Acharya and his personal hatred of the Raj. Yesterday you spoke of the goodness of Queen Victoria. I think it was never in your mind to attack the Raj, but only the Nizam. Rajeshwar Acharya intended to use you to advance his own personal revenges, and to lead you into war with the Raj." Ogilvie paused. "In so doing, Your Highness, he led many of your elephants to death and many to flight."

"Not so."

"I'm afraid it is so, Your Highness. It is a simple statement of fact." He added, "Queen Victoria herself would be upset at your loss."

Again the black eyes glittered, almost feverishly. "Queen Victoria rides upon an elephant?"

"No. She has carriages. But the elephant is high in her esteem. I say what I have said already: that the Raj would perhaps replace your losses."

The Rajah waved a hand in the air. "Am rich, with many rooms of diamonds, rubies, emeralds, gold. Can buy elephants. You seek to bribe, Captain sahib?"

"No." Ogilvie shook his head, then leaned forward, staring earnestly into the Rajah's face. "If the elephants were perhaps a personal gift from Her Majesty the Queen-Empress . . . a token to you of her esteem . . . would they not be more valuable than any elephants that riches could buy? Will you not consider this, Your Highness?"

"Gift from Queen Victoria?"

"Yes, Your Highness."

There was a long pause; then the Rajah said, "I consider, Captain sahib."

Ogilvie bowed his head, holding back a sigh of relief. Then he pulled out his watch. "Please consider quickly, Your

Highness. I have but two hours from the time I left my General. After that the guns will open."

"Not so."

"It is so, Your Highness. It is the word of my General."

The Rajah shook his head. "Still not so. Rajeshwar Acharya made preparations, all round the city, many weeks ago. Before one hour, if needed, all guns and soldiers and horses go pouf, pouf, pouf." He threw up his hands. "Vairy big bangs . . . what you say in your tongue, British soldiers are on top of minefield."

*　　*　　*

True words: they had been horrifyingly confirmed by an officer of the Rajah's military staff brought into audience for the purpose. The whole perimeter of the city had been mined to a depth of three-quarters of a mile, and the mines could be detonated by the simple pressing of a plunger in a small fortress-outpost on the city's fringes. Ogilvie pointed out to the Rajah urgently that the force now encamped outside was only a fragment of the army that was marching upon him from the Kistna River, with infantry and cavalry and many, many more guns. If the minefield was blown that evening, the oncoming troops would still arrive, would see the dead bodies of their comrades, and would annihilate Ranga-pore.

"I must talk to my General, Your Highness."

"If talk, General sahib will move men back. Then not go pouf, pouf."

"Neither will Rangapore, Your Highness." Ogilvie hurried over a weak point in his argument: if allowed time to think, the Rajah would realise that field guns covered a very wide area of fire. "Allow me to talk, to ask my General to withdraw his guns. It is in your own interest, Your Highness."

"And ask good Queen Victoria for elephants?"

Ogilvie nodded. "Yes, of course."

For a while longer the native ruler pondered, then reached a decision. He nodded vigorously, indicated that the Captain sahib could speak to his General sahib, but that the supply of elephants in considerable numbers by Queen Victoria would be a pre-requisite to any meaningful discussion on his own part. This made clear, he clapped his hands and, when a turbaned officer approached, spoke to him in his own dialect, rapidly and somewhat incoherently. After this Ogilvie was removed from the Rajah's throne chamber under guard and was led out through the palace gates and along the narrow alleys, past curious and hostile crowds held at bay by the ready rifles of the Rajah's soldiers, to the tower where the white-clad man had called from earlier. He climbed a spiral staircase to the top, where he looked out over the British lines beneath a sky darkening as the sun went down. Brilliant sunset colours lit the guns and the alert sentries and picquets. Behind them the plain lay immense and lonely, seeming to stretch back to the very frontiers of space. Ogilvie, standing in full view, called loudly. "This is Captain Ogilvie of the Royal Strathspey. I must speak to the Major-General at once on an urgent matter."

An acknowledging shout came back and at once Corcoran was seen moving forward from the lines with his ADC. "What is it, Captain Ogilvie?"

Briefly Ogilvie passed the word about the minefield, suggesting a withdrawal of a mile back.

"And blow up the damn city once I've done so!" Corcoran called back truculently. "If you were not at risk, I might well do that. Suppose I withdraw—then what? More parley?"

"Yes, sir. The Rajah knows the main body of men is on its way. I suggest delay." Ogilvie paused. "It would be of great help if I could promise elephants, sir."

"*What?*"

"Elephants."

"Elephants?" The Major-General sounded incredulous.

"Yes, sir. His Highness has a weakness for them. He lost a lot today—"

"They all buggered off, I suppose."

"Yes, sir, apart from the actual casualties. If Queen Victoria would send elephants—"

"*Queen Victoria?*"

"Yes, sir. A personal gift to His Highness. It would help, I assure you. May I have the authority, sir?"

There was a bellow of laughter, quickly stilled. The Major-General shouted back, "It's a small enough price to pay for saving British lives, Ogilvie. Yes, the authority is yours and will be honoured."

"Thank you, sir—"

"And Ogilvie—if it helps even further the buggers'll have the royal arms tattooed across their damn arses!"

*   *   *

Ogilvie listened for a moment to the orders for the withdrawal and was then escorted back to the palace. His Highness, although delighted by the promise of elephants, deferred final decision: Ogilvie was not permitted to leave the city. The Rajah went into private conference with his advisers and military staff; this conference lasted well into the night and when it was over no result was announced to Ogilvie, waiting under guard in a small chamber leading off the great hall of the palace. When His Highness emerged from his conference, Ogilvie was merely taken to the room he had occupied before, and locked in. Next day meals were brought, but there was no other contact with the outside world; and from his window, which looked out over the other side of the city, he had no view of the British guns. It was an isolated feeling and one that led to all manner of speculation: the Rajah might well be a great deal wilier than he appeared, the simpleton's approach to his problems could be but an act after all. Or he might not take the word of the Raj as expressed by Major-General Corcoran that elephants would be provided. He might defer all decision until Queen Victoria had made good the promise given in her name, in which case he, Ogilvie, might have many a week to kick his heels in solitude and nagging anxiety. The day dragged past interminably and moved into the succeeding night, and still no word came. By dawn Ogilvie had convinced himself that something had gone wrong, though he could not even make a reasonable guess at what it might be. He got up, ate breakfast brought by servants who would not utter, and thereafter paced his room, backwards and forwards, as he had done spasmodically throughout the previous day. But shortly after the many bells of the old city had rung for noon, his door was unlocked and the Rajah's major-domo beckoned him from the corridor.

"His Highness will see you, Captain sahib."

Ogilvie went out. He was taken, not to the throne room, but to a point on the outer walls of the palace, a point that looked easterly across the plain towards the Kistna River. His Highness was standing there, looking over the plain, an anxious yet hopeful expression on his face. He turned when he heard Ogilvie's approach.

"See!" He pointed. "You hear, yes?"

Very faintly, Ogilvie did hear: he heard the distant strains of the pipes and the beat of the drums sounding out over the still, close air. He approached the wall and looked to where the Rajah was pointing. Still a long way off there was an enormous dust-cloud spiralling up into the sky and rolling out to either side. There was a low but increasing rumble of many wheels, of guns and limbers, of Supply and Transport wagons, of field ambulances . . . all the varied noises and the panoply of a division on the march. As the column came nearer Ogilvie heard the pipes and drums more clearly, more stridently, and saw the splash of colour, the regular movement of the tartan of the Royal Strathspey leading the relief column towards Rangapore.

The Rajah spoke. "Was truth! British come. Raj come. I am good, good friend, Captain sahib." His tone was insistent. He clapped his hands together in a childlike gesture, then put them to his ears. "Flap, flap!"

"Flap, flap."

The Rajah raised an eyebrow, hopefully. "Bring elephants?"

"Patience, Your Highness."

*   *   *

The regiments and batteries and squadrons moved in, the very stuff of war and victory, completely surrounding the city beyond the limit of the mined perimeter, the pipes and drums playing the men to their stations. As the music stopped, Major-General Corcoran rode forward ahead of his Staff Officers, approaching the point where Ogilvie had been picked up two days before.

"A parley," he called out. "I come in peace to make negotiations with His Highness."

No time was lost now: men came out from the city, bowing to the representative of the all-powerful Raj. A hand was placed on the Major-General's bridle and he was led forward, disappearing into the maze of alleys. He was gone for a little more than two hours, and when he reappeared Ogilvie was with him. The returning party was met by Brigadier-General Masefield, mounted and saluting smartly.

"Well, sir?"

"Well indeed, Masefield, but I could do with a *chota-peg* to clear my nostrils of the stink. So could Ogilvie."

Masefield turned and shouted at no one in particular, "*Chota-pegs* for the General and Captain Ogilvie." Corcoran dismounted; almost by the time his feet touched ground a bearer had come with a tray and whisky and a soda siphon. Corcoran took his glass and cocked a sardonic eye at Ogilvie. "To Her Majesty's elephants, who've brought peace to the land!"

"To Her Majesty's elephants . . ."

The toast drunk, Corcoran took Masefield's arm. "When the newly arrived men have rested, we'll march out for the

215

Kistna and Secunderabad—a long way to go and a dusty one, but we're lucky not to have to sweat it out here."

"It really is peace, sir?"

Corcoran nodded. "I have the treaty—the draft documents, anyway. And His Highness has my word. It'll all need ratification by the Governor General in Council, of course . . . but it's peace all right, Masefield."

"Well, thank God for that." Masefield looked directly at the Major-General. "And Captain Ogilvie?"

Corcoran nodded; he understood the drift. "It's Ogilvie who brought about the peace. I'll be reporting that, I need scarcely add. In the meantime, he'll detach to the nearest railway station on our march for Secunderabad, and entrain for Ootacamund." A gleam came into the Major-General's eye. "He can carry the requisitions!"

Masefield lifted an eyebrow. "What requisitions, sir?"

"Why, the elephants. I've drawn up a requisition on old Farrar-Drumm. He'll enjoy foraging around for elephants— give him something to do!"

Eighteen

"ONE CAN TROT, canter and gallop, doncher know," Sir Clarence said, manipulating a lever at the side of the strange machine upon which he was seated. He began to jog up and down. "It quickens the circulation and stimulates the liver." On the base of the contraption the legend read: Horse Exercise For All. Vigor's Horse-Action Saddle As Used By HRH The Princess Of Wales. Brightens The Brain. "I've lost faith in leeches," Sir Clarence went on. "Can't cure damn rheumatics, don't know what they bother to qualify for! What?"

"No, sir."

"Well, anyway . . . about you, Ogilvie." Farrar-Drumm clambered off his instrument of torture, looking much relieved as he made his way to his desk. "You're halfway through a Court Martial, I suppose you realise?"

"Yes, sir."

"Failed to surrender yerself to military custody after yer escort was killed—serious, that, very. Puts me in a quandary, or would have, had I not received instructions from Calcutta. Don't do it again, though."

"No, sir."

"Sad about poor Nesbitt and his men, very. I don't like these deaths. Good feller—Nesbitt. Reliable. Still, I don't doubt, and no more does anyone else, that you did yer best. What?"

"Yes, sir. May I ask, sir, what instructions you had from Calcutta?" It was never safe to allow the Southern Army Commander to stray from the point for long.

"What? Oh yes, yes." Farrar-Drumm pushed papers

217

about on his desk. "His Excellency the Viceroy, in his capacity as Governor General in Council, y'know. Charges to be withdrawn. Charges, that is, of failure to surrender yer person to re-arrest."

"I see, sir. And—the others?"

Farrar-Drumm pursed his lips. "Officially the Court Martial is merely adjourned. The thing has to be gone through with, don't you see? A royal personage—it can't just be dropped, that's surely obvious."

"But—"

"No buts, Ogilvie. Buts and ifs don't exist on Her Majesty's service, we deal in present facts. The court will reassemble as soon as Lord Brora reaches Ootacamund."

"Lord Brora, sir? Is he to prosecute again?"

"Of course he is." Farrar-Drumm began to wheeze and then had an attack of coughing. When it was over he went on, "Lord Brora's almost fit again, so's Black who will act in command of yer regiment in Brora's absence here—or perhaps until Lord Dornoch rejoins, which I gather is to be quite soon now. But that's not for me to pronounce upon, since yer brigade's being despatched back to Northern Army in Peshawar." The General picked up a document deposited by Ogilvie on his arrival. "What's this?" He settled his eyeglasses on his nose. *"Elephants?"*

"Yes, sir—"

"Bless my soul—*hundreds* of 'em! Ridiculous. I haven't got any—that is, none to spare. Certainly not in such numbers! Has Corcoran taken leave of his senses, or what?"

Ogilvie said, "They're part of the peace treaty with the Rajah of Rangapore, sir, as I mentioned."

"Rangapore? Oh, that. Yes. Oh, very well, I suppose I shall have to pass on the requisition, but where the devil does one get so many damn elephants, may I ask?"

Ogilvie kept a straight face. "Queen Victoria, sir."

"Eh? Are you being impertinent, Ogilvie?" The heavy white eyebrows went up in outrage. "That was an irrelevant remark, was it not?"

218

"I think you'll find Her Majesty's name in the requisition, sir." Ogilvie coughed discreetly. "Sir, the Court Martial. Am I to—"

Farrar-Drumm held up a hand, peremptorily. "You shall be silent, sir, if you please! I spoke of formalities, or I'm almost sure I did. You must not be unduly anxious. Damn it, a wink's as good as a nod to a blind horse, what?"

* * *

Fresh depositions were made: Major-General Corcoran and Brigadier-General Masefield had words to add. General Farrar-Drumm remarked that no doubt this was irregular, but at least it served the all-important principle of justice and right which he held, he said, sacred. All the motions were gone through: a transcript of the proceedings, after vetting by the Viceroy acting in his capacity of Governor General in Council and as such supreme head of the Army in India, would need to be available to Whitehall for the perusal of Field-Marshal Lord Wolseley, Commander-in-Chief of the British Army, and of the Foreign Office, in addition to the Prime Minister and Her Majesty. German interest and German honour had of necessity to be satisfied. Farrar-Drumm read the final pronouncement: "The Court having carefully considered its verdict finds the accused Not Guilty of the first three charges but Guilty of the fourth, namely, that he did fail in his military duty to make a proper appreciation and reconnaissance of the position facing him on the night in question before entering the defile. The Court passes sentence of reprimand, which sentence is subject to confirmation by the Governor General in Council. The Court wishes to add a rider that in its view there was no dereliction of duty other than aforesaid that could have led to the unfortunate death of His Royal Highness Prince George of Hohenzollern."

Three weeks later, after the Viceroy's ratification of both verdict and sentence had been notified, Ogilvie made the

219

long journey to Calcutta to receive the official reprimand from the Commander-in-Chief, India, Sir George White. His father Sir Iain, in his capacity as Northern Army Commander, was also present, standing stiff and formidable beside the Commander-in-Chief.

The reprimand given stingingly, Sir George White stared at Ogilvie. "You have no complaint?"

"None, sir."

"Good." The Commander-in-Chief relaxed his face into a smile. "Sit down, Ogilvie."

"Thank you, sir." Ogilvie sat.

"Now, Ogilvie, you've done well, though I certainly don't condone breaking out of arrest. However, having said that, I will admit I don't know what might have been the result if you had not done so. You've been of much service to the Raj, and I'm grateful, and so is His Excellency the Viceroy. Trouble's been averted and I'm happy to say it appears as though the peace will last—"

"Subject to the arrival of the elephants," Sir Iain interrupted. "May I make a suggestion?"

White sighed. "Can you be prevented, Sir Iain?"

"With respect, sir, no I cannot." A devilish grin had started to play round the Northern Army Commander's mouth. "I have in mind employment for an officer of the 114th Highlanders . . . I understand Masefield does not propose uttering charges against Lord Brora for disobedience of orders. In this I shall concur. Brora has no damn manners, but then neither have I. He's not backward in action—and he has other virtues, however hidden." Sir Iain paused. "Are you aware of one of these virtues, sir?"

Sir George shook his head. "No, but don't let me stop you telling me."

The grin widened. "He is kind to animals, sir. He hunts them, but is kind. I suggest that when Her Majesty's gifts are ready to move, Lord Brora could be spared on temporary detachment to Rangapore for duties with the Supply and Transport?"